The Manx Cat

Marjan Swantek

With a chapter on genetics by
BARBARA PRESTON HAUKENBERRY.
Contributions by BARBARA ST. GEORGES and
KIM EVERETT (CFA all-breed judges), JANE HELLMAN,
and the late LEE SPAFFORD.

© 1984 Chanan

CAROL KYLE, EDITOR

Title page: Leslie Falteisek's CFA 1984 National winner, Clacritter Claudell, a dilute calico grand champion. Photo: Chanan.

Distributed in the UNITED STATES by T.F.H. Publications, Inc., 211 West Sylvania Avenue, Neptune City, NJ 07753; in CANADA to the Pet Trade by H & L Pet Supplies Inc., 27 Kingston Crescent, Kitchener, Ontario N2B 2T6; Rolf C. Hagen Ltd., 3225 Sartelon Street, Montreal 382 Quebec; in CANADA to the Book Trade by Macmillan of Canada (A Division of Canada Publishing Corporation), 164 Commander Boulevard, Agincourt, Ontario M1S 3C7; in ENGLAND by T.F.H. Publications Limited, 4 Kier Park, Ascot, Berkshire SL5 7DS; in AUSTRALIA AND THE SOUTH PACIFIC by T.F.H. (Australia) Pty. Ltd., Box 149, Brookvale 2100 N.S.W., Australia; in NEW ZEALAND by Ross Haines & Son, Ltd., 18 Monmouth Street, Grey Lynn, Auckland 2, New Zealand; in SINGAPORE AND MALAYSIA by MPH Distributors (S) Pte., Ltd., 601 Sims Drive, #03/07/21, Singapore 1438; in the PHILIPPINES by Bio-Research, 5 Lippay Street, San Lorenzo Village, Makati Rizal; in SOUTH AFRICA by Multipet Pty. Ltd., 30 Turners Avenue, Durban 4001. Published by T.F.H. Publications, Inc. Manufactured in the United States of America by T.F.H. Publications, Inc.

Contents

Foreword

I am writing this book for you and your Manx cat. It is a compilation of material from many Manx lovers the world over. As secretary of Manx International Breeders and Fanciers, I often received letters of inquiry, weekly, from readers as to where they could get a book about the Manx cat. I decided it was necessary to write one, so I have called upon many Manx authorities for their expertise in various areas. To them I am eternally grateful.

I was fortunate to find a publisher who also believed in the need for more information about our marvelous Manx breed. I am glad to add this volume to the growing list of books available to the cat fancy. I hope that you will find this book informative and helpful in understanding the Manx. Once you have let a Manx adopt you, you will never want to be without one.

It is not surprising that Manx are the dog lover's cat since dogs and Manx get along so well together. Here, reacting to a surprise development, Lupracan Mus Jamys Kyaghan takes refuge behind the canine members of his family, smooth Brussels Griffons Wildra's Chocolate Chip and Wildra's Godelieve van E, bred by Sandra Tetzlaff, and Australian Cattle Dog R-Bar-P's Cattle Kate, bred by Carol A. McCabe. Breeder: Mary E. Stewart. Owners: Barbara and Erika Haukenberry. Photo: D. H. Shagam.

Acknowledgments

My sincere appreciation to the following contributors: First, and foremost, to Janelle Preston, without whose assistance Manx Cats would never have been completed. Thanks also to Dr. Neil Todd of the Carnivore Genetic Research Institute; the late Dr. Douglas Kerruish, Inspector Bob Teare, the Honorable E. P. Dunne and staff, and Dr. Larch Gerrad of the Isle of Man; Dr. Martin DeForest of Guelph University; Martha Oldham and Blair Wright of Canada; Jane, Glen, and Sean Hellman of Wales; Franklin Boon of Holland; Mrs. L. C. McEwan of Australia; Barbara Preston Haukenberry; the late Lee Spafford; Charlene Beane; CFA judges Barbara St. Georges, Kim Everett, Mary Stewart, and Jim Lynch; CFF judge Bill Bryan; Samra Childers; Debi Allred; Connie Million; Susan Nuffer; Gail and Marlene Robinson; Irene Kertay; Marion Hall; Hazel Swadberg; Alice Hanbey; Sandy Tetzlaff; and Leslie Falteisek. Finally, thanks to *The Manx Cat, Cat Fancy,* and *Daphne Negus's Cat World* magazines, and to the CFA *Yearbook* . . . and, of course, thanx for Manx!

CHAPTER ONE

What is a Manx Cat?

The Manx cat, as far as we know, originated on the Isle of Man hundreds of years ago. It is there that the first records were found describing the strange tailless cat, which is believed to be a mutation of the island's domestic cats. Interestingly, the word *stubbin*, which means tailless cat, can be found in the Manx dictionary.

The Isle of Man is a fascinating place to study the frequency of genetic change in a domestic cat population. Its insularity provides a well-defined space, yet its geographic location in the middle of the Irish Sea leaves it potentially subject to diverse external influences. Although at one time the island was central in the Viking sphere of influence, it has since become increasingly affiliated with British political and commercial interests. What has remained constant is the interbreeding of tailless cats on this small island, and this has led to the reinforcement of the tailless factor as a predominant gene among the island's cats.

Currently, the human population on the Isle of Man is around sixty thousand, one-third of which lives in the port city of Douglas. The balance of the population is found in numerous towns and villages along the coast and throughout the island's interior. The island has no significant industry, aside from tourism, and its landscape may be characterized as rural and pastoral. Despite its small size and high standard of living, parts of the island are quite wild. The climate is surprisingly mild, and cats are able to find shelter the year 'round without human support. There are no barriers to movement about the island, and if any heterogeneity in cats

Above: The Isle of Man crown piece was last minted in 1970. Photo: F. E. Boon. **Below:** Visiting the Manx Breeding Cattery in Noble Park, Douglas, Isle of Man, is the author, Marjan Swantek. Photo: Brian Doyle.

Above: Isle of Man judge Bob Teare at the Royal Manx Show in Castletown, Isle of Man. Photo: Marjan Swantek. **Below:** Heathlands Charlie in Foxdale, Isle of Man. Photo: Marjan Swantek.

exists, it must be due to man's intervention. The total pet cat population is roughly fifteen thousand, of which five percent are "fancy" cats and immigrants. This five percent is not allowed to roam freely, and most have been surgically sterilized; hence, there seems to be no threat of their interbreeding with the indigenous population of Manx cats.

APPEARANCE AND PERSONALITY

Besides taillessness, the Manx cat has other unique features that make it stand out in the cat world. It has full, rounded cheeks that give it a jowly appearance, as well as an outward-turned earset that resembles the rocker of a cradle. The Manx neck is short and thick, and the shoulders arch back to a high, rounded rump, which is supported by a pair of long hind legs. When viewed from the side, the cat's back is short and its flank is quite deep. A heavy, double coat of fur covers its strong, compact, solidly-built body. "Rumpies" are completely tailless and have an indentation at the base of the spine where a tail would normally begin, while "stumpies" (also known as "stubbies") sport a mere stump of a tail. A "riser" falls somewhere between the rumpy and stumpy types; it is a Manx that has a small piece of bone or cartilage at the end of its spine, and sometimes it is referred to as a "rumpy riser." Then of course there are tailed Manx. A pair of Manx parents could produce a litter of kittens whose tails are of varying lengths (a rumpy, two stumpies, and a tailed, for instance) but that same pair might produce all tailed offspring in the next litter.

The late Dr. Kerruish of the Isle of Man said that breeding Manx was like reaching into a bran barrel . . . you never know what you'll get each time. So it seems! This is why, incidentally, you don't see too many true Manx (that is to say, completely tailless Manx) at cat shows, as only rumpies and risers can be shown for championship. Stumpies and tailed Manx may be shown in the AOV, any other variety, class.

What is the personality of the Manx like? As with most breeds, this varies with individual cats and with some particular lines of Manx. Basically, their temperaments resemble the people of the Isle of Man—quiet but active, shy but friendly, witty but reserved, clever but trusting. A study in contradictions. If you have never lived with a Manx cat, then you have missed a great experience. Like most shorthaired breeds, they are active and very hardy. They are affectionate in their own way and form close attachments to their owners. Manx will accept the total family they adopt, but they will choose one individual as their special person. Once a Manx surmounts its birth trauma, it is strong, healthy, and can be kept both indoors and out in all kinds of weather. Many males are still siring at a ripe old age, and females have litters at the age of ten. Both male and female take an active part in caring for their young.

Manx are clever cats that love to play games with you. If you don't provide them with toys of their own, they will make, or steal, their own. I have often thought that they should play basketball with the Boston Celtics, as they are great on rebounds! They love to engage you in a game of handball as well, and they are also good at hockey, soccer, and other sports. Manx like to fetch for you; that is why they are sometimes called the "dog lover's cat." Many owners, in fact, say that Manx remind them of dogs. If you don't keep up the fetching game, they will remind you with a tap on the leg, or by dropping the object in your coffee cup or some other "appropriate" place, that it is your turn. As far as fetching is concerned, they may even fetch the dog across the street. They are apt to jump on the dog's back and give it quite a scare. With dogs they know, however, they are quite friendly and will play just like a puppy. They truly are playful cats at heart.

FOLKLORE

There are a number of legends that attempt to explain the origin of the Manx breed. One fable tells of a tailless cat that arrived in 1588 with the Spanish Armada. The truth is, there is no record of this, nor of tailless cats in Spain. Then there is the rumor that Manx came from the Far East on board ship. There are Japanese Bobtails in Japan, but these cats have a twisted, bobbed tail that, according to Dr. Neil Todd, is genetically different from that of the Manx. Probably the most attractive story surrounding the origin of our breed involves Noah and the Ark. It seems Noah had two tailed (normal) cats that were playing outside the Ark. When he called them to come on board, the two cats just ignored him, saying, "Oh, *traae dy liooar*" (time enough) and kept right on playing. Finally, when they did come aboard, Noah was just slamming the door shut and he chopped off their tails by mistake.

Another myth about why Manx cats have no tails comes from the period of Manx history when the Scandinavians invaded the island. As these intruders tried to slice off the native cats' tails so that they could adorn their helmets, all of the mother cats panicked and promptly bit off their kittens' tails so that the warriors could not steal these priceless "decorations." There is also the tale about Samson, who swam the Irish Sea just for exercise. When he swam past the Isle of Man, a cat caught him and nearly drowned him with its tail. Samson quickly chopped off the cat's tail in defense, and it has never had one since.

There is a verse handed down from an unknown source that Manx folk tell about their tailless cats.

> Noah, sailing o'er the seas,
> Ran high and dry on Ararat,
> His dog then made a spring and took
> The tail from off a pussycat.
> Puss, through the window, quick did fly
> And, bravely, through the waters swam,
> And never stopped 'til high and dry,
> There, upon the Isle of Man.
> The tailless earned Mona's thanks,
> And, ever since, was called a Manx!

Whichever you choose to believe, that the Manx evolved as a mutation of the domestic cat or that it emerged through myths and superstitions, you won't be disappointed if you let a Manx cat own you. You will say, "Thanx for Manx!"

ISLE OF MAN CATTERIES

On the Isle of Man, in Noble Park, just above the capital city of Douglas, there is a government-operated cattery that was established to preserve native Manx cats. Since visitors to the island were stealing Manx, which they considered to be "lucky" cats, Dr. Douglas Kerruish decided to design an indoor breeding establishment that would give thirty Manx cats and kittens permanent and comfortable housing. At the same time, he hoped to create a tourist attraction where Manx cats could be seen at their best. Many of the resident kittens have made their way from the cattery (located at Knockloe Farms) to the United States at one time or another. One of the first to be exported was Manninagh Mona, who was sent to William Bryan in Hatboro, Pennsylvania. At age ten, she was a consistent finalist as a grand premier. Mona was a lively brown tabby. Another notable Manx, Manninagh Katedhu (a black with a white locket), was on the payroll of the British Home Office where she received a wage of five shillings as "Official Mouser."

There are two other catteries on the Isle of Man: Bob Teare runs the MSPCA shelter, where Manx kittens can be seen, at Ard Jerkyll Farm in East Foxdale, and Roy and Sandra Whiteside oversee the Heathlands Cattery in that same area. Theirs is one of the nicest indoor/outdoor catteries that I have ever visited. They also have Manx and Cymrics (long-haired Manx) of their own, and one of their male Manx even has a CFA registration. It's a small world after all.

CHAPTER TWO

Genetics and the Manx Cat

Barbara Preston Haukenberry

M anx cats originated from a mutation which probably occurred on the Isle of Man hundreds of years ago. Tailless kittens still occasionally appear in litters of other breeds, and the Japanese Bobtail, a breed which resulted from the action of a different gene mutation that also shortens the tail, is well established. Therefore, it is clear that spontaneous mutations which effect tail length are continually occurring among cats. Spontaneous mutations, unless they are clearly beneficial to the organism, tend to die out, so Manx lovers should be grateful that the Manx mutation occurred on an island which geographically protected and limited its breeding population of cats, thereby allowing the Manx mutation to gain a foothold and to flourish. This geographic isolation also was responsible for the development of the unique Manx personality which, to the pet owner, is of even more importance than physical type.

BREEDING CHALLENGES

Although the study of Manx genetics may initially seem to be quite complex, it is well worth the effort. Anyone considering breeding Manx should be aware of the negative, as well as the positive, effects of the incompletely understood Manx gene. Manx breeders are a dedicated, hardy lot who are willing to risk their time, money, and emotions in exchange for seeing the joy that a pet kitten brings to its new home or for seeing that special show Manx shine in the ring. In breeding

Manx, does the good outweigh the bad? Manx breeders will answer that question with a resounding "Yes!"

Although the Manx is considered to be one of the most unusual of all the cat breeds, technically it is not a breed. Unfortunately, kittens that inherit the Manx gene (M) from both of their parents (MM) do not survive and probably die during an early stage of development in the uterus. As a result, Manx litters are usually smaller than those of normal cats. The kittens that do survive are either heterozygous (Mm) and have inherited only a single Manx gene from one parent and a normal gene from the other or kittens that have inherited normal genes from both parents (mm). The former show a variation in tail length that ranges from a complete absence of tail (rumpy) to a partial tail (stumpy), while the latter have full tails. Therefore, Manx can never breed true since it is impossible to produce a living kitten that has two Manx genes (MM). It is unclear whether the dominant Manx gene, itself, is lethal or whether it is not, but instead is closely linked to a recessive lethal gene. Linkage with a recessive lethal in some ways seems to be a better way of accounting for the fact that kittens that are heterozygous for the Manx gene usually survive while kittens that are homozygous never survive.

Since the Manx gene is a dominant gene, kittens that inherit it will exhibit shortening of their tails to a greater or lesser degree. Only the kittens that do not inherit the Manx gene will have full tails. It is extremely important to remember that the cat fancy considers a tailed Manx to be a purebred and just as much a Manx as one that has a shortened tail or the complete absence of a tail. In fact, tailed and docked tailed Manx are often shown in the AOV (Any Other Variety) class along with stumpies and Manx with rises that are too long for championship competition. Only the rumpy, rumpy riser, and showable riser Manx may compete in the championship classes, but the longer tail lengths are recognized in AOV because of their contributions to Manx breeding programs. Important attributes such as ear set, head type, boning, and coat are determined by genes which are not affected by the Manx gene.

The various tail lengths of Manx carrying the Manx gene are the result of variable expression of the gene which, in turn, is due to modifiers which determine how much of the tail will be absent. This accounts for the wide variation in the number of vertebrae absent from individual kittens carrying the Manx gene even though they may be from the same litter. Only a small percentage of Manx kittens are rumpies. Also, at times it seems as if the rump receives conflicting genetic messages and extra skin will be produced where a full tail would be on a normal cat. This can range from an excess of skin, sometimes filled with cartilage, at the end of a stumpy's partial tail to a tiny, hollow, vestigial "tail" of skin hidden in the fur of a dimpled (rumpy) Manx. To confuse things even more, there have been reports, although rare, of tailed Manx being bred together and producing kittens with shortened tails. These exceptions to the rule may have been due to the misclassification of stumpies with very long stumps as tailed Manx, but they may also have been the result of incomplete penetration of the Manx gene.

Although the dimpled rumpy is considered to be the ideal Manx, scientists quite rightly consider manx with all or part of their tails missing to be deformed cats. Some Manx lovers counter this scientific fact with the amusing, but appealing, argument that Manx are simply higher on the evolutionary scale and therefore more advanced than ordinary cats. After all, humans lost their tails during the evolutionary process. Actually, scientists consider a large number of different breeds of different species to be deformed. The short muzzles of the Persian cat and the Pug dog, the folded ears of the Scottish Fold cat, and the size of miniature horses are greatly admired by fanciers, yet they are considered to be defects by scientists. Unfortunately, the Manx gene does have defects other than a shortened tail connected with it, and these can be quite serious. Again, the Manx is not unique in this. Persians can have missing tear ducts and excessive tearing, Bulldogs are sensitive to heat and have malocclusion, Scottish Folds can have skeletal abnormalities, and some toy dogs have such fragile bones that they can break a leg merely by jumping off a low wall. Manx breeders are well aware of the problems that can be caused by the Manx gene, but they realistically accept their losses as a necessary evil in their constant efforts to continue and to improve the breed.

Serious defects associated with the Manx gene usually occur in the rumpy. Breeders tend to limit their rumpy-to-rumpy breedings over successive generations and they periodically breed rumpies to tailed Manx or to stumpies in an attempt to lower the number of defective kittens born. This is not to say that breeding a rumpy to a tailed Manx will avoid producing defectives; it will not, since any cat carrying the Manx gene may produce them.

Manx defects affect the spine and the hindquarters. Besides taillessness, another defect, curvature of the spine, is also bred for since the standard calls for the back to arch from behind the shoulders, as opposed to a normal cat's level back. Other defects are not so benign, and since they may take some time to appear, many breeders will not sell a rumpy Manx until it is three-to-four months old. Manx kittens may be born with neurological defects. They may develop megacolon due to improper passage of the feces through the colon, which results in the feces distending the colon at some point and blocking it. They may, on the other hand, have urinary and/or fecal incontinence and be unable to control the elimination of their excreta. There may be weakness of the hindquarters which may affect both hind legs or only one. The hind legs may be so severely affected that a kitten will be unable to move them independently and will have a gait much like a rabbit's hop. These kittens, naturally, are called "hoppers." If the weakness affects only one hind leg, it may be so subtle as to be noticeable only when the cat or kitten makes a sharp turn.

Fusion of vertebrae is extremely common among Manx, but it usually has no adverse effects. However, some Manx have a twisted spine which throws the hips out of alignment. Kittens are sometimes born with spina bifida, which is due to a protrusion of the spinal cord, and a bubble can often be seen at the site. Kittens may also be born with the anus missing and others may develop rectal prolapse, in which part of the rectum protrudes through the anal opening.

Above: Supreme Gr. Ch. Swady Dena Megan of Cleomar. Breeder/owner: L. Alice Hanbey. Photo: Jal Duncan. **Below:** An excellent example of a Manx, according to the standard, is Gr. Pr. and Ch. Lupracan Mus Kherree Kayt. Breeder: Mary E. Stewart. Owner: Barbara Haukenberry. Photo: Brooks Institute of Photography.

Although the Manx gene is associated with multiple defects, a kitten or cat bought from a responsible breeder will be healthy and strong. Responsible breeders euthanize defective kittens and no ethical breeder will put a defective Manx, even if it has only a very minor defect and is in every other way a superb example of its breed, in the show ring! It should be made clear, however, that young Manx do tend to have touchy digestive systems and occasional bouts of diahrrea are common. This *does not* mean that one has a defective Manx, since the tendency is usually outgrown.

COLOR AND PATTERN GENETICS

An interesting area of Manx genetics concerns the inheritance of coat color and pattern. The Manx is a cat of many colors, and often it is useful for a breeder to know the colors and patterns which can result from a breeding. Gene pairs, carried on the cat's nineteen chromosome pairs, determine the phenotype and the genotype of a cat. The *phenotype* refers to what a cat looks like, while the *genotype* refers to what a cat is genetically, including those characteristics that it is not showing but which it can pass on to its offspring. Gene pairs, called *alleles*, have the same locus or position on the chromosome pairs and only the individual genes in each pair can be dominant or recessive to each other. A *dominant* gene blocks the expression of a recessive gene and a *recessive* trait only appears when a recessive gene matches up with one like itself in the gene pair. A cat is *homozygous* for a trait when both of the genes in its gene pair for that trait match, and it is *heterozygous* for the trait when it has one dominant gene and one recessive gene in the gene pair. One knows that a cat is carrying a recessive gene when it exhibits, phenotypically, a dominant trait yet produces a kitten with a corresponding recessive one. Also, if a cat is homozygous for a recessive trait, its offspring will all at least carry that recessive characteristic. Dominant genes are represented by capital letters (*i.e.*, B), recessive genes are represented by lower case letters (*i.e.*, b) and a dash (—) represents an unknown gene in the gene pair. The following is a list of the Manx color and pattern genes along with their genetic symbols:

A agouti
a non-agouti
B black
D dense
d dilute
I inhibitor
i non-inhibitor
O orange
S white spotting
s non-white spotting
T mackerel tabby
t^b classic tabby
W white
w non-white

Since females have two X (female) chromosomes, their genetic symbol is XX. Males have one X chromosome and one Y (male) chromosome, so their genetic symbol is XY. Black and orange (the latter is called red in the cat fancy) are different from the other genes on the list because they are sex-linked and they are only carried on the X (female) chromosome. Therefore, B and O also may indicate the X chromosome as well as color. Whether a male cat is black or orange is determined by a single gene which is inherited from his dam. The genetic symbol for a black male is BY; for an orange male it is OY. A female can inherit a gene for black or orange from both of her parents, and since B and O have different loci on the X chromosome, neither one is dominant to the other. A female, as a result, can be black (BB), orange (OO), or tortoiseshell (BO). The mixed black and orange of the tortoiseshell, which is always female unless there is a genetic accident, is the result of those colors appearing only in the areas which are affected by their corresponding genes. Dense and dilute merely determine whether a cat is black (BBD— or BYD—), blue (BBdd or BYdd, the dilute of black), orange (OOD— or OYD—), cream (OOdd or OYdd, the dilute of orange), tortoiseshell (BOD—), or blue-cream (BOdd, the dilute of tortoiseshell).

White is often mistakenly referred to as being dominant. This is not true since it has its own locus. White masks the other colors and a homozygous white cat (WW) will only produce white kittens, although the other colors will still be present in the genotypes of the parent and its kittens. A heterozygous white cat (Ww) will produce colored as well as white kittens.

The *inhibitor gene* is a dominant which determines the amount of pigment in the hair and which has its greatest effect on the less dense areas of color, such as between the stripes of the silver tabby. *Polygenes* probably modify the action of the inhibitor gene. Colors are produced that range from the silver and cameo tabbies, which show the least suppression with the darkest tipping, to the shaded silvers, chinchillas, shaded cameos, and shell cameos, which have the least amount of colored tipping. Smoke (either black or blue) and silver tabby are the colors produced by the inhibitor gene which are most often found among Manx. The lighter colors are very rare because Manx usually do not have the necessary polygenes. Since the inhibitor gene (I) is dominant to the non-inhibitor gene (i), a smoke kitten, for example, must have at least one smoke parent. However, smoke kittens have appeared in litters from black-to-black matings. This is due to modifying genes which cause the smoke undercolor to vary greatly from very light to very dark, dark enough for the smoke parent to have a phenotype which is virtually indistinguishable from that of a black cat.

All cats, including solids, have two tabby genes. There are three types of tabby markings, but only the striped mackerel and the blotched classic types appear in the Manx. Mackerel tabby (T) is dominant to classic (t^b) and a cat's pattern, whether expressed visually or merely carried in the genes, is determined by its tabby alleles. Solid cats often show their tabby pattern in the form of "ghost striping," (a barely visible pattern), especially when they are kittens. Whether or not a cat is a solid or a tabby depends on its being agouti or non-agouti. The *agouti* gene (A) produces ticking in between the stripes of the tabby pattern and produces the tabby cat. The *non-agouti* gene (a) removes the ticking from between the stripes and a solid color cat (the color of the stripes) is the result. The non-agouti gene, even though it is recessive to agouti, masks the expression of the tabby pattern when a cat is homozygous for non-agouti.

An exception to the rule that a tabby cat must have at least one agouti gene is the orange tabby. Since the agouti gene bands the hair between the tabby stripes so that they are yellow with black tips and an orange cat has no black, an orange tabby can either be agouti or non-agouti. The two types are indistinguishable. Also, a solid red cat is either a mackerel tabby which has been bred to have as few and as pale markings as possible or it is a classic tabby which has been bred for tabby markings which are as braod and patchy as possible. The latter type is usually found among longhairs.

There is great variation among white-spotted cats, and scientists generally recognize ten grades of piebald white spotting ranging from grade 1, a completely colored cat, to grade 10, a completely white cat. More than one gene may be involved, but it is probable that most of the spotting is due to a single and probably semi-dominant gene. *Semi-dominant* means that the heterozygote (Ss, in this case) differs from the homozygote (SS) in appearance. It is thought by many that the heterozygote has less white spotting than the homozygote. However, they undoubtedly overlap and there is great variation, either genetic (due to polygenes) or developmental (due to individual idiosyncracy), among individuals, especially heterozygous ones, and even among different lines.

Genetic checkerboards are an accurate means of predicting the results of breeding the different colors and patterns which have been discussed. They show what results are possible and the odds for or against getting them. However, the ratios which they produce are ideal and the more complex checkerboards, especially, require a large number of kittens before the paper results and the actual breeding results approximate each other. There is also a size limitation to checkerboards. One pair of genes for each parent results in a four-box checkerboard, two pairs result in sixteen boxes, three pairs result in sixty-four boxes, and four pairs result in two hundred fifty-six boxes. Using one, two, or three gene pairs at a time is the most practical approach, even if more than one checkerboard must be worked out in order to find out the results of the combinations of several gene pairs.

Probably the best way to begin with the checkerboards themselves is with the tabbies, ignoring color. Since all cats carry two tabby genes, even when breeding a solid to a tabby, it is often helpful to know what tabby genes the solid is carrying. The solid parent's tabby genes will pair off with those of the tabby parent and they will affect the patterns, either expressed or merely carried, of the kittens that result from the mating. Two homozygous mackerel tabbies, (TT) and (TT) bred together will produce all homozygous mackerel tabbies. Two homozygous classic tabbies, ($t^b t^b$) and ($t^b t^b$) bred together will produce all homozygous classic tabbies. A homozygous mackerel tabby (TT) bred to a homozygous classic tabby ($t^b t^b$) will produce all mackerel tabbies carrying the classic tabby gene (Tt^b).

A homozygous mackerel (TT) bred to a mackerel carrying classic (Tt^b) will produce the following:

Tt^b (mackerel carrying classic)

		T	t^b
	T	TT	Tt^b
TT (mackerel)	T	TT	Tt^b

Ratio—1:1. 1 mackerel (TT), 1 mackerel carrying classic (Tt^b).

A mackerel carrying classic (Tt^b) bred to a classic ($t^b t^b$) will produce the following:

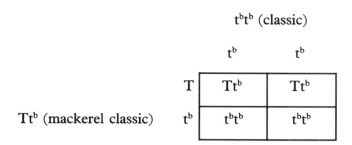

$t^b t^b$ (classic)

		t^b	t^b
Tt^b (mackerel classic)	T	Tt^b	Tt^b
	t^b	$t^b t^b$	$t^b t^b$

Ratio—1:1. 1 mackerel carrying classic (Tt^b), 1 classic ($t^b t^b$).

A mackerel carrying classic bred to another mackerel carrying classic will produce the following:

Tt^b (mackerel carrying classic)

		T	t^b
Tt^b (mackerel carrying classic)	T	TT	Tt^b
	t^b	Tt^b	$t^b t^b$

Ratio—1:2:1. 1 mackerel (TT), 2 mackerels carrying classic (Tt^b), 1 classic ($t^b t^b$).

The ratios given above for the mackerel and classic tabby genetic combinations are correct for any combination of a single gene pair. For example, a black female carrying dilute (aaBBDd) bred to a black male carrying dilute (aaBYDd) will produce the same ratio as shown under the last checkerboard: 1 black (aaBBDD or aaBYDD), 2 blacks carrying dilute (aaBBDd or aaBYDd), and 1 blue (aaBBdd or aaBYdd). When both parents are homozygous for the same trait, the gene pairs for that trait can be dropped because all of the kittens will also be homozygous for that trait. Therefore, in the black-bred-to-black example, one can ignore the first two gene pairs (aa and BB or BY) because they are the same for both cats, except for sex, and one can use the third checkerboard, merely substituting D for T and d for t^b. Since a female is XX and a male XY, the ratio for the sex of a litter of kittens is 1:1, the same ratio as in the first checkerboard. Sex only needs to be taken into account when both black and orange are in a checkerboard, since, as mentioned, these colors are sex-linked and only carried on the female (X) chromosome.

The following is an example of a two-gene–pair checkerboard, although three gene pairs are given. However, since both cats are homozygous for non-agouti, the first gene pair (aa) can be dropped since all of the kittens will also be homozygous for non-agouti. This will simplify the checkerboard and save time and space.

A tortoiseshell carrying dilute (aaBODd) bred to a black carrying dilute (aaBYDd) will produce the following:

aaBYDd (black carrying dilute)

		BD	Bd	YD	Yd
	BD	BBDD	BBDd	BYDD	BYDd
aaBODd	Bd	BBDd	BBdd	BYDd	BYdd
(tortoiseshell carrying dilute)	OD	BODD	BODd	OYDD	OYDd
	Od	BODd	BOdd	OYDd	OYdd

Ratio—2:1:1:2:1:1:2:1:1:2:1:1. 2 tortoiseshell females carrying dilute (aaBODd), 1 tortoiseshell female (aaBODD), 1 blue-cream female (aaBOdd), 2 black females carrying dilute (aaBBDd), 1 black female (aaBBDD), 1 blue female (aaBBdd),

CFA National alter winners Gr. Pr. and Ch. Nufurs Nu Newdell, bred by Susan Nuffer and owned by Gail Robinson, and Gr. Pr. and Ch. Gaeylyn of Castletown, bred by Martha Jones and owned by Marjan Swantek. Photo: Chanan.

2 orange males carrying dilute (aaOYDd), 1 orange male (aaOYDD), 1 cream male (aaOYdd), 2 black males carrying dilute (aaBYDd), 1 black male (aaBYDD), 1 blue male (aaBYdd).

Genetic checkerboards are not only interesting, but they also allow a breeder to breed for color as well as for type. Although *type* (how well an individual Manx conforms to the breed standard) should be of paramount importance, it cannot be ignored that breeders often do have color preferences. A knowledge of basic feline color and pattern genetics and an understanding of how to work simple checkerboards can add much to the enjoyment of breeding the wonderful Manx cat.

CHAPTER THREE

Tatleberry Cattery Study

Jane Hellman, owner of Tatleberry Cattery in Wales, did a prolonged study to help her decide which male and female breeder cats to keep in her Manx program. Having had good success with certain cats, and, having gained the Supreme Royal Cat of the British Isles title in her Tatleberry Long John Silver (quite a feat for any Manx cat!), she carried out the study for her own interest.

Several years ago the American Manx Club conducted a similar study and the conculsion was that there is a wide variation in tail lengths, which occur as a result of a great many breeding strategies. In particular, the study indicated that the use of stumpies in breeding programs seemed to produce a higher rate of stumpy offspring. One of the more favorable breeding combinations was the longy/rumpy matings, which produced a fairly split litter of rumpies and longies but no stumpies or "half-tails."

Of course, just when we think we have prediction of tail length down to a science, something unexpected pops up— so it is with Manx cats. In Manx, it is very difficult to predict, with any certainty, tail length. Studies, like the one done at Tatleberry and the one done by the AMC, are valuable to *all* Manx fanciers. If you conduct your own study, by keeping records of your stock and your breeding patterns, we urge you to share your results!

The following diagrams and Classification of Manx Cat Types were submitted to us by breeder Jane Hellman, and we are delighted to share this information with you.

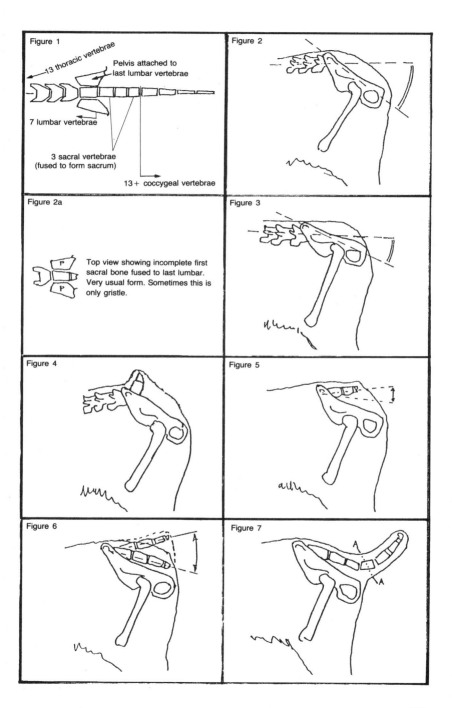

Figure 1

13 thoracic vertebrae

Pelvis attached to last lumbar vertebrae

7 lumbar vertebrae

3 sacral vertebrae (fused to form sacrum)

13 + coccygeal vertebrae

Figure 2

Figure 2a

Top view showing incomplete first sacral bone fused to last lumbar. Very usual form. Sometimes this is only gristle.

Figure 3

Figure 4

Figure 5

Figure 6

Figure 7

29

CLASSIFICATION OF MANX CAT TYPES

Figure 1 portrays the top view of the relevant parts of the normal spine. *Figures 2 and 2a* represent the rumpy, a cat that has no complete sacral vertebrae; frequently the first one is present, but it is incomplete and fused to the last lumbar vertebra. In *figure 3* the roundness of the rump is affected by the angle of attachment of the pelvis. *Figures 4, 5, and 6* portray the rumpy riser. There are three types of risers identifiable. In our experience, the rarest is figure 4, the "fixed" rise. This is a section of sacral bones fused in a vertical position. As it is immovable, apart from spoiling the roundness of the bottom, it will "stop the hand." (cf. CFA Manx Standard). In figure 5 we see perhaps the most common form of the riser. This diagram shows two complete and one incomplete sacral vertebrae, which are fused together and which can be raised and lowered from the junction with the last lumbar vertebra. This type can have just an incomplete vertebra, as in figure 2a, which, if it moves, must be considered a riser. These are eminently showable cats in this respect. Figure 6 is basically the same as figure 5 but with all three sacral vertebrae plus an incomplete coccygeal one, which are also movable in the same way. Although the angular movement is the same, because of the extra length the vertical movement is greater, thereby again spoiling the roundness and interfering with the hand as it is run down the back. In some cats even when the rise is relaxed it makes a noticeable bump in the skin. These cats are not of show standard type. These last two types of riser (figures 5 and 6) can be very difficult to detect on the bench, as some cats will clamp it down because of shyness with strangers or fear of the unfamiliar surroundings. Sometimes scratching the cat on the last two lumbar vertebrae encourages it not to lift any rise but also to take its "stand." A judge of course does not have recourse to X-ray equipment and so must judge the cat by feel. This does not mean a finger poked up the bottom. *Figure 7* is everyone's idea of a stumpy. However, a stumpy can have no more vertebrae than shown in figure 6, but because the skin is shaped around the bone as in AA in figure 7, it becomes a stumpy. This is important, because such a cat is definitely not show quality and again is hard to detect on the bench.

Some thoughts regarding the longy: Where a stumpy ends and a longy begins is a matter of personal decision, as a longy is a long stumpy. But the definitive difference between a longy and a full-tailed cat of Manx parentage, however long the longy's tail is, is that the last coccygeal vertebra present is distorted and the cat carries the Manx gene. Some cats possess a flap or patch of thickened skin where the tail would begin. Unless this is associated with coccygeal vertebrae, it cannot be considered a stump, although it may very well spoil the apperance of the roundness of the bottom and thereby lose as many points.

Lupracan Mus Tillie of Nufurs, the first Manx Distinguished Merit in CFA. Breeder: Mary E. Stewart. Owner: Susan Nuffer. Photo: William Nuffer.

CHAPTER FOUR

Choosing and Caring for a Manx Cat

If you purchase a kitten from an established Manx breeder, you are apt to get a healthy, hardy animal. Cat shows are a great place to meet breeders, but if you can't get to one, ask a local veterinarian for a breeder referral. If you know that a particular breeder has shown Manx, then you can be assured that the kitten you purchase has been well cared for, has had its inoculations, has a pedigree, and has met the requirements of showing and of having been raised in a healthy environment. The walls inside a cattery don't have to be loaded with ribbons won at shows as evidence that it produces good pets, but this does show a certain level of achievement toward meeting the Standard for the breed.

Look at the kitten's parents, if they are available, to see what your cat may look like at maturity. And be sure to check not only the kitten's temperament but each of its parents' temperaments as well, since temperament traits are inherited to some degree. Select an alert, bright-eyed animal, one that is the picture of good health. Some Manx are active and energetic, while others are quiet and shy—both can be found in the same litter. Choose the Manx personality that suits you and your lifestyle. Many people fall in love with the runt of the litter, and while these fragile little creatures may require more attention during their first few weeks of life than their healthier, stronger littermates do, they *can* grow into self-assured cats that are faithful companions.

A typical Isle of Man Manx, Douglas of Peel. Photo: F. E. Boon.

Before making your purchase, check the kitten's ears. Inside the ears there may be a little wax (a smooth, tan coating), but there should not be dark, granular matter, as this may indicate the presence of ear mites. The kitten's eyes should be free of discharges, though occasionally a kitten may have a small "sleep crust" in the corner of its eye. You should also check the kitten's teeth, which should be clean and white (and sharp!).

FEEDING

Feeding your kitten a variety of nutritionally complete foods will help keep it in good health. There are canned products with a high moisture content which are especially palatable; semi-moist packaged foods with even less moisture content; and dry foods with little or no moisture content at all. This last group can be left out at all times as snack, but cool, fresh water should also be made available. Dry foods help keep the cat's teeth in good condition; the grinding action works like a toothbrush and helps keep plaque and tartar from building up on the teeth and getting out of hand. Even if you supply dry foods for your Manx, it might be wise to take your pet to a veterinarian who can clean and scale the cat's teeth periodically.

Remember that each Manx is an individual and may have special dietary needs. I have certain cats that are susceptible to gingivitis (inflammation of the gums), and I find that an increased dosage of vitamins B and C help their condition. Pregnant queens, weaned kittens, sick cats, older cats, and cats with allergies or special health problems may require changes in their diets. Of course it is best to check with the veterinarian first.

I feed my Manx raw meat with supplements and dry food with a low ash content. I add a very small amount of my own vitamin/mineral powder to their food, as well as oatmeal, parsley flakes, salt, and calcium ascorbate (a vitamin C source). I often supplement their diets with cheddar cheese (which they seem to crave) and cottage cheese for kittens.

GROOMING

When grooming your Manx, use a stiff, rubber-tined brush and a fine-toothed flea comb. Yes, part of your cat's regular grooming routine may, at some time, include the removal of fleas from your pet and its environment. I prefer flea powders to flea sprays, and I also use an ultrasonic pest control device as well. Plastic mitts with mesh pockets in front, into which flea powder is poured, are also available. The mitt is a convenient way of patting flea powder into your cat's fur. Most of these products are available at pet shops and they are important grooming aids to have on hand. No matter how clean and healthy your Manx is and no matter how sanitary its environment is, fleas are bound to show up sometime—they can bother most warm-blooded animals, humans included.

Daily brushing is important, but if you stroke your pet often, you may be able to limit brushing to just once a week. If your Manx is shedding, you may want to brush the dead hair out so that as the cat licks and grooms itself it will be less likely to swallow loose hair. Manx shed their winter coats during hot weather, and they may shed during reproductive cycles or if they are nervous or stressed.

Claw clipping is an important ritual. I begin clipping my kittens' claws at four weeks of age so that they become used to the process. I do this once a week with claw clippers made especially for cats. I place the kitten on my lap and begin by extending a paw. I press on one claw until it is unsheathed; then I begin to clip. I am careful to take off only the pointed end of the claw, because if I were to cut too deeply into the pink area, it would bleed. This procedure is repeated for each claw. Clipping, by the way, is not a permanent condition, as the claws will grow in again. Regular clipping will help keep the claws dull. I do not recommend declawing cats, and, in fact, I will not sell one of my Manx cats to anyone who plans to have their pet declawed either.

CAT FURNITURE

When considering the environment in which your pet will live, you will want to invest in some safe cat furniture.

Whether you buy or build a "cat tree," be sure that it is sturdy and secure at the base so that it will not tip over. Even those that stand upright by means of a spring-pole should not be top heavy; otherwise they may topple like timber when a twelve pound Manx lands on them. Manx will tackle anything—bolted down or otherwise—and they can be very athletic at times. Some floor-to-ceiling structures have shelves for perching on and boxes for hiding in, which are attached to the center post. Some have hammocks for snoozing in, while others have enticing toys that hang from strategic locations. Floor-to-ceiling cat trees can be made with carpet remnants fastened over plywood, particle board, or whatever else seems sturdy to you. Nubby-tufted or looped-pile carpeting are recommended as coverings. Rough-textured upholstery material is also suitable. Shag carpeting is not desirable, as claws can get stuck in the long carpet strands. My Manx like a low, ground-level tunnel or an A-frame structure to hide and play in and to climb over and sharpen claws on.

Keep in mind that cat trees and hideaways are not necessarily replacements for your furniture, draperies, and carpeting. Your Manx may decide to stretch out and claw these things for some reason, even though you have provided the cat with its own resting places and scratching surfaces. With practice and patience on your part, however, you can teach your cat to scratch against its *own* furniture and to learn what is "off limits" in your home. As mentioned before, I find declawing (the surgical removal of claws) cruel and unnecessary. Better to provide appropriate scratching surfaces and train your Manx to use them.

Manx also like a cozy bed to curl into. Check your local pet shop, where you will find a variety of cat beds from which to choose.

If you keep several Manx, you may need to invest in a cat run or pen, rather large enclosures which can be kept indoors or outdoors in warm weather. Make certain the run or pen is placed where there is adequate ventilation and light. These enclosures can figure importantly if you need to house a breeding queen and stud, a queen and her kittens, a stud cat, or a sick cat.

TOYS AND PLAYTHINGS

Manx provide a great relationship for everyone, regardless of their age—just ask anyone who owns or who has owned one. Manx are marvelously adaptable to their owner's needs and moods; they are intelligent, entertaining, sympathetic, and sincere. You will have endless fun playing together, especially if you invest in or make a few toys. When purchasing toys for your pet, be sure to choose safe ones. Avoid plastic toys with small parts that can break or fall off and get stuck in the cat's throat. Pet shops can recommend safe toys for your Manx.

Ping pong balls are an endless delight, as are soft rubber balls. Even cotton balls can be fun for a Manx to pounce on and "kill." Although they are hard to find these days, rabbit's foot charms are much appreciated by Manx cats. In fact, anything made of fur or fake-fur is sure to cause a stir. Fresh or dried catnip and catnip-filled toys are favorites. I sprinkle dried catnip around the house and sit back and watch the various responses it gets. Some Manx like to roll in it, others eat it, and a few—usually younger cats—will ignore it. Old socks or stokings can be filled with catnip and will provide great fun. Most Manx, I have found, love to chase after a braid of yarn that has been fastened to a stick. By waving the stick around, you can encourage your pet to exercise . . . until your arm gets tired, that is.

If you don't supply your Manx with a few toys, it will probably steal something of yours! They love socks and will carry them around just to have a ready toy. They are mad about paper wads or anything with which they can play hockey. As a matter of fact, they are pretty happy with anything that they can move around . . . so let your imagination run wild as you dream up games for you and your Manx to play.

A WORD ON HOUSEPLANTS

Plants can be a hazard to your cat's health. Certain greens are safe to keep around, but be sure that they are the right variety. Learn to identify the plants and shrubs that are harmful to cats, like Dieffenbachia, Philodendron, Azalea,

A blue and white bi-color stumpy queen, Evette, of the Granvale Cattery, Queensland, Australia. Owner and photographer: Mrs. L. C. M. McEwen.

and Oleander, just to name a few. Most cats will not chew on these, but then again some just might. Why take the risk? Putting the plants up high out of a cat's reach is no solution, as some Manx are like mountain goats when it comes to scaling heights.

You can grow your own greens to satisfy your pet's urge to chew on plants. Some cats need to chew on greens to help them purge an occasional hairball (a wad of hair) that forms in the digestive tract as a result of the constant licking of fur. Sometimes I put parsley, quite sparsely, into their raw meat mix—this seems to help add greens to the diet.

CHAPTER FIVE

Naming Your Manx Cat

For those of you who would like to give your fabulous feline a Manx Gaelic name, here are a few from the *Cregeen Manx Dictionary* and *Lessoonyn ayns Chengey ny Mayrey Ellan Vannin* (Lessons in Manx Gaelic). The names are listed alphabetically.

Aalin	—beautiful
Aarkey	—from the sea
Aigh-vie	—good luck
Ainle	—angled
Amlee	—seaweed
Argid	—silvery
Arrane	—song
Ballaglonney	—Fairy bridge
Ballawhane	—witch
Bane	—white
Bannaught	—confident
Banshee	—she-devil
Barrey	—barred
Beg	—small
Ben–varrey	—mermaid
Bog	—soft
Boggey	—joy
Bollan	—charm
Booleybane	—warlock
Braar	—brotherly
Bracken	—brindled
Breck	—spotted
Bree	—energy

Brod	—choicest
Bun	—heavy bottom
Bun-ny-gaeyee	—eye of the wind
Caardys	—pedigreed
Cadd	—defender
Caghlaa	—changeable
Cam	—crooked, twisted
Cammey	—flexible
Carrey	—friend, crony
Carrick	—fortress
Caslys	—likeness
Cassan	—pathway
Cassee	—curling, bending
Cass-olley	—new growth
Catreeny	—Catherine
Chairn	—lord
Chamoo	—neither, nor
Chelleeragh	—direct
Chibbyr	—spring, well
Chipp	—whip
Chonning	—rabbit
Clea	—gateway
Cleaynee	—alluring
Cormid	—equal
Correy	—seedling
Creeney	—provident
Cronk	—a hill
Cronney	—fate, destiny
Creg	—a rock
Daaney	—bold, daring
Dean	—a goal, mark
Dedge	—clever
Deigan	—he-devil
Dhone	—brown
Dirk	—dagger
Doo	—black
Doolish	—Douglas
Dorrin	—storm, tempest
Ellan Vannin	—Isle of Man

Erskyn	—above
Farrane	—fountain
Feer chreeney	—very wise
Feer vanney	—blessed
Fer-toshee	—foremost
Fey	—fathom
Feyyerrey	—lasting
Firriney	—truth
Foddey	—far, distant
Foylican	—butterfly
Frea	—giving
Fys	—knowledge
Fy-yerrey-hoal	—at long last
Gaey	—wind
Gaeylyn	—of the coals
Gaidee	—frisky
Garrey	—your friend
Garroo	—rough
Gheyr	—very dear
Ghlass	—grey-blue
Gialdyn	—promise
Giare	—short
Gien	—cheerful
Glen	—pure
Goll-twoaie	—rainbow
Gorrym	—blue
Griannagh	—sunny
Guilley	—a boy
Hannah	—already
Harroo	—bull
Hollyssid	—brightness
Hoptunaa	—Halloween
Huggey	—to and fro
Jannoo	—satisfy
Jerk	—hopeful
Jerkyl	—expected
Jerragh	—direct
Jerree	—last
Joarree	—strange

Kay	—misty fog
Kayragh	—darkness
Keayn	—ocean, sea, or kind
Keear-lheeah	—mottled grey
Keilly	—witty
Keimach	—prancer
Kemmyrk	—protector
Kionan	—a lump
Leagh mooar	—precious gift
Lhiannan-shee	—blythe spirit
Maccan	—little son
Mannan	—sea god
Margey	—fair
Markym-jeelym	—heat wave
Marrey	—the sea
Meecheelagh	—silly soul
Mhellia	—harvest doll
Mian	—eager
Moirrey	—Mary
Molley	—sweetness
Mooir-lheeney	—flood tide
Moyllychairn	—hallelujah
Mynney	—fine
Myrgeddin	—likewise
Neddrym	—heavy
Noa	—new
Nollick	—Christmas
Phynnodderee	—mischievous troll
Ruy	—reddish
Scadoo	—shadow
Shareid	—superior
Sharroo	—bitter
Sheayn ny mae	—peace be with you
Shee	—peaceful
Shynney	—love
Smaragaeyn	—cinders
Soderick	—sunny creek
Sonney	—plentiful
Spyrryd	—spirit

Four-month-old Cleomar Bear Essence of Kowala in a charming pose.
Breeder: L. Alice Hanbey. Owner: Candi Oglenski. Photo: Roger Michael.

Sy gansy moorey	—pebbly beach
Taggloo	—talkative
Tarroo	—bull
Tehi-tegi	—beautiful enchantress
Traae dy liooar	—time enough
Trean	—valiant
Tushtey	—intelligent
Vaney	—white and bright
Veg	—little
Vooralagh	—haughty, aloof
Wingjeear	—leader, foremost
Yeearree	—desire, wish
Yindys	—wonderful

CHAPTER SIX

Traveling with Your Manx Cat

Most cats don't mind traveling. There are a few that may prefer to stay at home, but most of them would rather be with their "person." For the protection of your pet, you should provide a suitable carrier or cage. There are various sturdy plastic carriers available in different sizes, as well as collapsible models that fit into most station wagons and that are safe enclosures, especially if you are planning to stay in a motel. If you are planning a long trip, a litter box and food containers will be needed, as well as food, drinking water, paper towels, and a few cat toys. Some cats get carsick, although most travel without difficulty. The cat needs to see out of the car window and it must have fresh air. If the carrier is to be in direct sunlight part of the time, you may wish to drape something over it so that it will be shaded. Most cats are quite comfortable in an air-conditioned car.

If you are staying in motels (and this is usually the case if you're traveling to a distant cat show), you will need a collapsible cage and a sheet of plastic to protect the motel room's floor covering, which often is carpeting. Avoid turning your Manx loose in a motel room; there are many dangers that you may not be aware of. You may not see the "escape" hole in a wall or in a cabinet that can lead to the cat's being entrapped in a wall space. And don't forget to keep all doors to the room closed, since any curious cat can dart out the door in a flash. Check all window screens; pets have been known to escape through screened windows that were not secured. Keep the motel bathroom door closed so that your Manx cannot be exposed to various bathroom cleansers. Whenever you plan to leave the motel room, keep the cat in its carrier or cage and place the Do Not Disturb sign on your door.

When traveling, it makes sense to take along the type of food your cat is accustomed to, as well as bottled water from home. Water varies by area and it is not a good idea to upset your cat's digestion at this time. Whenever I go to a cat show or on a long trip, I often take along a supply of baby food meats, as they are a high-quality protein source and easy for cats to digest.

If you plan to travel by air, there are small carriers that fit under the passenger seats; however, I recommend a more flexible type of carrier, one that is made of canvas and carried like an athletic bag. It should be large enough for your Manx to stretch out in and it should have ventilation holes. If you do plan to take the cat on board with you, you must notify the airline far enough in advance. Sometimes they allow only *one* cat in the passenger section and it might as well be yours, if this is what you desire. Do not allow your pet to be sent through the X-ray machine before boarding the plane; have the animal checked separately. If you do not plan to take the cat on board the airplane, it can ride quite comfortably in its carrier in the pressurized baggage compartment.

If you ever need to ship a cat (a breeding queen, or a kitten going to its new home), contact several air carriers and check their prices, as they do vary. You will need to fill out a health form for the transport of a live animal, or you may have to furnish the airline with a health certificate from your veterinarian. These documents are usually valid for ninety days, and they state that the cat is healthy and has had its required inoculations. Most airlines are experienced in handling the shipment of animals and their regulations are similar from one carrier to another; however, it is best to check out all of this information well in advance.

Most cats can travel by air without first being tranquilized, unless of course your veterinarian recommends this. If he

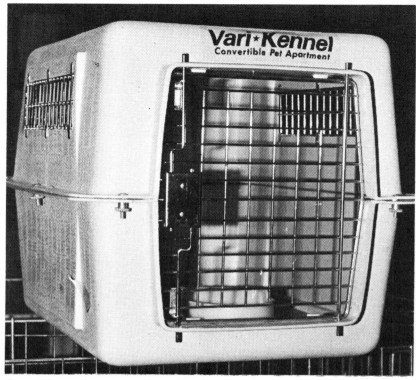

One of the various types of carriers for transporting your cat. Photo: Courtesy of Doskocil Manufacturing Company, Inc.

does, you may want to administer the tranquilizer a few days or so before the big trip to see just how your Manx responds.

If you plan to ship your Manx or travel with it from one country or continent to another, make it a point to become familiar with the various quarantine regulations . . . these vary from place to place in different parts of the world. In most European countries, you can send cats directly. In Great Britain, Australia, and on the Hawaiian Islands, there is a quarantine period of several months. Keep in mind that any cat going to these areas should be old enough to withstand long quarantine periods. Some quarantine facilities house both dogs and cats, while others keep canines and felines separated.

CHAPTER SEVEN

Showing Your Manx Cat

Some of us started out with Manx pets and somehow got talked into showing our cats by other fanciers. The show scene is a world of its own—exciting, exhausting, and rewarding all at the same time—and it can be a new adventure for Manx owners. I have always felt that it is important to consider a cat's feelings toward cat shows. If the animal truly resists being shown or does not show well, or if it is off weight, out of condition, or does not feel well, it should stay home. Remember always to keep the cat's best interests at heart; after all, a cat show should honor your Manx cat, not your ego.

Cat shows help people who are not associated with the cat fancy learn about, appreciate, and enjoy felines. Most people find the shows interesting and fun. At cat shows various breeds can be promoted to their fullest extent, and an exhibitor can learn a great deal by comparing his cat with others of its kind, by listening to the judges, and by talking with other breeders and exhibitors. It has always been a thrill for me to see *any* Manx win, especially since our breed is considered to be a minority breed, but interest in Manx cats is growing and I believe we are making great progress in educating the public about our terrific tailless friends.

The best advice I can give with regard to showing your Manx at its peak of perfection is to talk with experienced Manx breeders and ask for their assistance. They will be glad to suggest grooming tips, to recommend diets, and so on. Don't hesitate to ask questions.

In preparing your Manx for a cat show, you will need to perform a few grooming procedures, such as brushing the coat thoroughly, clipping the claws, cleaning the ears, and brushing the cat's teeth (if your Manx will let you). Additionally, you will need to give your Manx a bath. Some Manx do not mind being bathed, while others will let you know very quickly how they feel about being immersed in water. Now, it is one thing for a Manx to play in a basin of water, near a tub full of bubble bath, or with a dripping faucet; however, it is quite another thing for these cats to be bathed deliberately! I prefer to bathe my cats as close to show time as possible, perhaps a few days in advance of the big event. Sometimes I use a flea shampoo or flea dip in addition to the application of regular shampoo, and sometimes I wonder why I even bother. It seems that no matter how free of fleas my cats are before the show, they frequently manage to come home with these pesky parasites.

There are various color shampoos and rinses on the market, made especially for cats, that will enhance the coat colors you are working with. Normally I breed Manx that are solid black (with a sable tinge). To darken the coat, I use a black hair color shampoo. A blue rinse can then be used effectively to add sparkle. With tabbies, I have often used my own pH-balanced shampoo. Some cat-show exhibitors like to use a coat gloss as a final touch, rubbing it into the cat's coat with the hands.

After the bathing ritual, the cat should be patted and rubbed dry with a rough-textured towel. It is extremely important to keep a cat that has just been bathed warm so that it doesn't become chilled and catch a cold. Some Manx do not object to your using a hair dryer to speed up the drying process, but others have a fit and make a prompt exit. If you do use a hair dryer, select a medium setting; avoid too high a setting, as this could burn the cat's skin, especially if you hold the hair dryer close to the cat. I like to use a heat lamp so that the cat's coat can dry naturally. I brush out most of the moisture first, and, of course, the cat's own tongue helps in this matter also. When the cat is dry to the bone, I brush and comb the fur. After a thorough brushing and combing,

CFA judge Sylvia Fitzgerald displaying her Best Kitten, Castletown Daffy-down Dilly. Breeder/owner: Marjan Swantek. Photo: Citrus Cat Club.

I run an anti-cling strip (like the ones used in clothes dryers) across the cat's fur to help eliminate static electricity, particularly when the air is dry.

On the day of the show, plan to bring along some supplies from home. You will need some type of covering for the show cage in which your Manx will spend most of its time (cage sizes are usually listed in the show rules and regulations), some clips to hold the cage covering in place, a litter box, food and water dishes, and perhaps a few toys to keep your Manx happy. The top and three sides of the show cage are usually covered. Some people decorate their cats' cages with curtains and quite elaborate trimmings; however, a large bath towel or a bolt of fabric can do the job just as well. Clothespins, metal clamps, or plastic clips work well to secure the cage covering. You might want to place a small rug in the bottom of the cage for your cat's comfort. Or you might decide to bring along a small cushion or pillow or even the cat's bed for your celebrity to curl up on. Make certain the cage is well ventilated, and keep in mind that most Manx prefer cooler temperatures.

Bring along a supply of litter (some shows may supply this), as well as food and water from home for your cat. Water from strange locations might not sit well with your pet, so it is best to be prepared with your own. Some exhibitors remove the litter pan from the show cage because their cats cuddle into them. If this is the case with your own cat, simply remove the litter pan and carry your cat to the pan for brief visits as needed. This way the cage will stay cleaner, since litter cannot be scattered about. And don't forget to pack a few grooming tools—a brush, a comb, a box of tissues, paper towels, and cotton swabs for last minute touchups. Even a Manx that is immaculate may need some last minute help so that it looks its very best in front of the judges. Before you leave home make certain to clip the cat's claws and to clean its ears. Don't wait until you are in the show hall to do these things. Your Manx will be more relaxed at home, whereas it may become excited and restless in a noisy show hall.

A number will be placed on top of your cat's cage. Listen carefully when numbers are announced so that you will know when the Manx Class is about to be judged. Be ready to bring your cat into the ring when it is called. If it is difficult to hear numbers being called, refer to the show schedule. Withhold comments during the judging; if you wish to ask questions of the judge, wait until he or she is finished judging to do so.

You may want to share the cost of a grooming space with another exhibitor. It is a good idea to secure space for this purpose, and it also makes a nice lunch spot. I use part of the space to display promotional material about the Manx breed.

Your cat may be lucky enough to win in various categories (which are based on sex, color, coat pattern, and so on) in the Manx Class; if so, it will go on to higher classes of competition. But no matter what the outcome of the cat show you attend, you should come home a *gracious* winner or loser, for even if your Manx does not win a ribbon or an award, it will have been a fascinating experience. There will have been much to learn. Once the show bug bites, you may find yourself busy almost every weekend of the year. And win or lose, don't forget to praise your cat after each show for a job well done.

If you want to enter a cat show, it is suggested you contact one of the many national cat registries or breed clubs for more information.

Quad. Gr. Ch. Cleomar Teddy Bayer. Breeder/owner: L. Alice Hanbey.
Photo: Roger Michael.

CHAPTER EIGHT

Judging the Manx Cat
Kim Everett, CFA all-breed Judge

Personally, I feel that the Manx Standard is excellent. In fact, it is one of the best Standards written and quite easy to interpret. One can easily get a mental picture of what a top quality Manx should be.

Many Manx may stand and walk well on the judging table, while others do not perform in this manner. Since the Standard does not specify *where* the cat shall walk and stand properly, we must assume that movement in the judging cage, as well as on the table, will be acceptable. We might see a Manx make a bee-line across the show hall while judges are "turning them loose" to observe them walk and stand properly. Manx don't often walk casually down the boardwalk, as they are very fleet of foot. Before disqualifying any Manx under this section, I would make every attempt to determine if the cat had a defect and actually could not stand or walk. Muscle structure and boning can reveal a lot. You have to work with some Manx to get them to stand. If I were a Manx and someone handled me roughly while checking my lack of tail, I would not wish to stand either. A judge can check a rounded rump with the palm of the hand. It is completely unnecessary to dig and root around. I like to tickle the back a bit, and this usually gets them to stand nicely. Allowing for a rise at the end of the spine is something that all judges should be aware of and not penalize for. On occasion a Manx will have a skin flap, not containing bone, at the end of the spine. This, too, should not be faulted.

I do not fault a solid color Manx for a locket, and the cat should not be penalized for this unless the locket is very large. Any breed, in which a locket is allowed, should be judged on its merit as a solid color and for type and coat alone. No standard should be interpreted at the whim of a judge, especially if the judge does not even raise the particular breed in question.

Manx hate to be stretched out, as we do with some breeds, and they look horrible in that position. They are so compact that they look best with their feet on the ground. If a cat were dropped from a height of a few feet, it could be injured. This is one breed that does not appreciate being tossed about. The Manx is a powerful cat and relies on good balance. As a Manx stands before you on the judging table, you can check its breadth of chest, heaviness of leg bone, shortness of back, the ear set and shape, and contours of the head. I always look for the "rocker" between the ears. This I find most often in mature males. It really sets off the head. I think that the Manx is a breed where the head alone will not put it up, as the overall total balance is so important, plus a well-padded coat.

I have long been a believer in beautiful grooming to enhance a cat. With today's competition as it is, everything counts to give a cat an edge. I see absolutely nothing wrong with trimming the hair hanging off the rump of the Manx to enhance its rounded rump. Exhibitors trim the inside of the ears on Abys and Siamese, and pluck the tail hairs on Persians to make the tail look shorter. Adding color, excess powder, and the like is another matter. Enhancing nature, however, is all right.

I guess I have always loved the Manx. They are more powerful looking than any other breed, and they are very unique. They have a somewhat aloof personality, but they show well and can be playful. The Manx really "turn me on." They are simply *all cat*. I have never bred or owned a Manx, but I am fortunate, as a judge, that I am able to handle so many beautiful Manx.

My first introduction to the Manx was through Loretta Willwirth Baugh. This was before I went into the judging program. At the time I was showing my Grand Champion Pharoh Rameses II. Loretta had called and asked if I would agent her beautiful black female, Kattidid. When Kattidid arrived in her spacious carrier, my husband Bob and I couldn't wait to get it open and see what she looked like. We opened the carrier and two copper eyes peered at us. Then she hopped out and proceeded to investigate our living room. She was just about the most beautiful cat I'd ever seen. She had a deep, lovely, double coat that shimmered, and she had a very short back. Loretta kept insisting that Kattidid wasn't perfect, and I doubted that. She looked terrific to me, as we had nothing of that quality in our area at the time. We took her to a Seattle show, where she did very well. She was really a show girl. Hammed it up at every opportunity. Big Red, or Rameses, also a ham, had competition that weekend. We did learn how Manx hop and pace, with a gait unlike any other cat. They were beauty in motion. We were sad when Loretta lost Kattidid, as she was a real beauty.

That was many years ago, and since that time the quality, in all colors, both male and female, has been outstanding. I often put several Manx in my finals. This tells me that the quality is surely there. All I can conclude with is congratulations to the breeders of this marvelous breed on the work that has been done to perfect the Manx to what it has become.

THE MANX STANDARD

Following is the Cat Fanciers' Association (CFA) Standard for Manx cats, and we include it here because CFA is recognized the world over and it is the largest of the cat registering organizations. Each cat registering association develops its own set of Standards, one for each of the breeds it recognizes for championship. A Standard is a written description of what an ideal cat should look like, in our case what an ideal Manx should look like. Each Manx is judged according to how well it measures up to its breed Standard; Manx are not judged against each other. Judges use the Standard to help them make their decisions in the show ring, and breeders strive to meet the Standard set forth for the breed . . . they strive to create cats that come as close to perfection, in terms of their type and temperament, as possible. There is no perfect cat, and there never will be. But the Standard can be viewed as a goal, something to work toward in improving our beloved Manx breed. Incidentally, the CFA Manx Standard is used not only in the United States (including Hawaii), but in Japan as well.

MANX

Point Score

Head and ears...25
Eyes 5
Body 25
Taillessness 15
Legs and feet.. 15
Coat 10
Color and markings... 5

GENERAL: The overall impression of the Manx cat is that of roundness; round head with firm, round muzzle and prominent cheeks; broad chest; substantial short front legs; short back which arches from shoulders to a round rump; great depth of flank; and rounded, muscular thighs. The heavy, glossy double coat accentuates the round appearance. With regard to condition, the Manx presented in the show ring should evidence a healthy physical appearance, feeling firm and muscular, neither too fat nor too lean. The Manx should be alert; clear of eye; with a glistening, clean coat.

HEAD AND EARS: Round head with prominent cheeks and a jowly appearance. Head is slightly longer than it is broad. Moderately rounded forehead, pronounced cheekbones, and jowliness (jowliness more evident in adult males) enhance the round appearance. Definite whisker break, with large, round whisker pads. In profile there is a gentle nose dip. Well-developed muzzle, slightly longer than broad, with

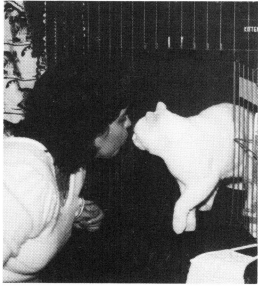

Above: Dagdas More Pounce Per Ounce. Breeder/owner: Patricia Raby. Photo: Chanan.
Below: Manx usually enjoy cat shows, as can be seen by this photo of Gail Robinson and Gr. Ch. Glen Maye's Gee Whiz. Breeder/owner: Gail Robinson. Photo: Marjan Swantek.

Above: The Manx gene can affect even mixed breeds, as is shown by this Siamese/Manx stumpy companion cat, Calli. Photo: Marjan Swantek. **Below:** A nicely marked Dutch Manx, Int. Ch. Sumark van't Huys Buytensorgh. Breeder/owner/photographer: F. E. Boon.

a strong chin. Short, thick neck. Ears wide at the base, tapering gradually to a rounded tip, with sparse interior furnishings. Medium in size in proportion to the head, widely spaced and set slightly outward. When viewed from behind, the earset resembles the rocker on a cradle.

EYES: Large, round, and full. Set at a slight angle toward the nose (outer corners slightly higher than inner corners). Ideal eye color conforms to requirements of coat color.

BODY: Solidly muscled, compact and well-balanced, medium in size with sturdy bone structure. The Manx is stout in appearance, with broad chest and well-sprung ribs; surprisingly heavy when lifted. The constant repetition of curves and circles gives the Manx the appearance of great substance and durability, a cat that is powerful without the slightest hint of coarseness. Males may be somewhat larger than females. Flank (fleshly area of the side between the ribs and hip) has greater depth than in other breeds, causing considerable depth to the body when viewed from the side. The short back forms a smooth, continuous arch from shoulders to rump, curving at the rump to form the desirable round look. Shortness of back is unique to the Manx but is in proportion to the entire cat and may be somewhat longer in the male.

TAILLESSNESS: Absolute in the perfect specimen, with a decided hollow at the end of the backbone where, in the tailed cat, a tail would begin. A rise of the bones at the end of the spine is allowed and should not be penalized unless it is such that it stops the judge's hand, thereby spoiling the tailless appearance of the cat. The rump is extremely broad and round.

LEGS AND FEET: Heavily boned, forelegs short and set well apart to emphasize the broad, deep chest. Hind legs much longer than forelegs; with heavy, muscular thighs and substantial lower legs. Longer hind legs cause the rump to be considerably higher than the shoulders. Hind legs are

Swady Cali-Q. Breeder: Hazel Swadberg. Owner: Lee Spafford. Photo: D. H. Shagam.

Above: Jamys loves playing with his Tuffy Mouse. Photo: D. H. Shagam.
Below: L. Alice Hanbey's adorable group of seven-week-old kittens. Photo:
Roger Michael.

straight when viewed from behind. Paws are neat and round, with five toes in front and four behind.

COAT: Double coat is short and dense; with a well-padded quality due to the longer, open outer coat and the close, cottony undercoat. Texture of outer guard hairs is somewhat hard; appearance is glossy. Coat may be thicker during cooler months of the year.

TRANSFER TO AOV: Definite, visible tail joint. Long, silky coat.

SEVERELY PENALIZE: If the judge is unable to make the cat stand or walk properly.

DISQUALIFY: Evidence of poor physical condition; incorrect number of toes; evidence of hybridization.

Manx Colors

WHITE: Pure glistening white. *Nose Leather and Paw Pads:* Pink. *Eye Color:* Deep blue or brilliant copper. Odd-eyed whites shall have one blue and one copper eye with equal color depth.

BLACK: Dense coal black, sound from roots to tip of fur. Free from any tinge of rust on tips. *Nose Leather:* Black. *Paw Pads:* Black or Brown. *Eye Color:* Brilliant Copper.

BLUE: Blue, lighter shade preferred, one level tone. Sound to the roots. A sound darker shade is more acceptable than an unsound lighter shade. *Nose Leather and Paw Pads:* Blue. *Eye Color:* Brilliant Copper.

RED: Deep, rich, clear, brilliant red; without shading, markings, or ticking. Lips and chin the same color as coat. *Nose Leather and Paw Pads:* Brick Red. *Eye Color:* Brilliant Copper.

CAPTIONS FOR COLOR PLATES 1 TO 16.

Plate 1
Above: Brown classic tabby, Shelleo Jessica. Breeder/owner: Shelly Page. Photo: Jal Duncan. *Below:* Quad. Gr. Ch. Cleomar Tinkerbelle. Breeder/owner: L. Alice Hanbey. Photo: Chanan.

Plate 2
Above: Supreme Gr. Ch. Cleomar Bonnie Eloise. Breeder/owner: L. Alice Hanbey. Photo: Chanan. *Below:* National Gr. Ch. Clacritter Claudell, a dilute calico. Breeder/owner: Leslie Falteisek. Photo: Chanan.

Plate 3
Above: Gr. Ch. Cilgerran Cymro Taffy. Breeder/owner: Kay A. Cullen. Photo: Chanan. *Below:* National Gr. Ch. Mendocino Bearelegance of Mayflower. Breeder: Pam Donohue. Owner: Muriel Slodden. Photo: Chanan.

Plate 4
Above: Supreme Gr. Ch. Swady Manix. Breeder: Hazel Swadberg. Owners: Susan and Gary Dirks. Photo: Chanan. *Below:* National Gr. Ch. Briar Brae Merphy. Breeder/owner: Barbara St. Georges. Photo: Chanan.

Plate 5
Above: Gr. Ch. Twilshire's Bit O'Honey. Breeder: Robin Maring. Owners: Irene and Bella Kertay. Photo: Donna Coss. *Below:* Ch. and Pr. Lupracan Mus Jamys Kyaghan. Breeder: Mary E. Stewart. Owners: Barbara and Erika Haukenberry. Photo: D. H. Shagam.

Plate 6
Gr. Ch. Lupracan Mus McNamara, a red mackerel tabby. Breeder: Mary E. Stewart. Owner: Susan Nuffer. Photo: Jal Duncan.

Plate 7
Above: Gr. Ch. Shelleo Benjamin. Breeder/owner: Shelly Page. Photo: Jal Duncan. *Below:* Ch. Clacritter Beau. Breeder/owner: Leslie Falteisek. Photo: Chanan.

Plate 8
Above: A cute six-week-old kitten at his first photographic session. Photo: Roger Michael. *Below:* Compare the difference between the dilute calico kitten on the left and the calico on the right. Photo: Roger Michael.

Plate 9
Above: Manx are usually good travelers. Kherree is ready to go to her next cat show. Photo: D. H. Shagam. *Below:* Like other cats Kherree loves a cozy box. Photo: D. H. Shagam.

Plate 10

Above: Shelleo Jessica. Breeder/owner: Shelly Page. Photo: Jal Duncan. *Below:* National Gr. Ch. Sinleo White Irish of Shelleo. Breeder/owner: Shelly Page. Photo: Bill Reach.

Plate 11

Above: National Gr. Pr. Gaeylyn of Castletown. Breeder: Martha Jones. Owner: Marjan Swantek. Photo: Chanan. *Below:* Kherree finds her A-frame a refuge from the world. Photo: D. H. Shagam.

Plate 12

Jamys and Kherree play peek-a-boo in their cat tunnel. Photo: D. H. Shagam.

Plate 13

Above: Quad. Gr. Ch. Manawyddan Pyramus of Marathon, a Cymric. Breeder: Solveig Pfluger-Smith. Owners: Joe and Samra Childers. Photo: Jack Nelson. *Below:* Supreme Gr. Ch. Swady Fanchet. Breeders/owners: Linda and Clarence Swadberg. Photo: Jal Duncan.

Plate 14

Above: Tr. Gr. Ch. Cleomar Cing Clone. Breeder/owner: L. Alice Hanbey. Photo: Roger Michael. *Below:* Tra Mar SS Mist, a stumpy. Breeder/owner: Marion Hall. Photo: Chanan.

Plate 15

Above: Gr. Ch. Arrows Mon Ami of Nufurs. Breeder: Linda Morse. Owners: Linda Morse and Susan Nuffer. Photo: Chanan. *Below:* Cleomar Irish Dancer. Breeder/owner: L. Alice Hanbey. Photo: Roger Michael.

Plate 16

Gr. Ch. Twilshire's Bit O'Honey. Breeder: Robin Maring. Owners: Irene and Bella Kertay. Photo: Donna Coss.

PLATE 1

CREAM: One level shade of buff cream without markings. Sound to the roots. Lighter shades preferred. *Nose Leather and Paw Pads:* Pink. *Eye Color:* Brilliant Copper.

CHINCHILLA: Undercoat pure white. Coat on back, flanks, and head sufficiently tipped with black to give the characteristic sparkling silver appearance. Legs may be slightly shaded with tipping. Chin, stomach, and chest are pure white. Rims of eyes, lips, and nose outlined with black. *Nose Leather:* Brick Red. *Paw Pads:* Black. Eye Color: Green or Blue-Green.

SHADED SILVER: Undercoat white with a mantle of black tipping shading down from sides and face from dark on the ridge to white on the chin, chest, and stomach. Legs to be of the same tone as the face. The general effect to be much darker than a Chinchilla. Rims of eyes, lips, and nose outlined with black. *Nose Leather:* Brick Red. *Paw Pads:* Black. *Eye Color:* Green or Blue-Green.

BLACK SMOKE: White undercoat, deeply tipped with black. Cat in repose appears black. In motion the white undercoat is clearly apparent. Points and mask black with narrow band of white at base of hairs next to skin, which may be seen only when fur is parted. *Nose Leather and Paw Pads:* Black. *Eye Color:* Brilliant Copper.

BLUE SMOKE: White undercoat, deeply tipped with blue. Cat in repose appears blue. In motion the white undercoat is clearly apparent. Points and mask blue with narrow band of white at base of hairs next to skin, which may be seen only when fur is parted. *Nose Leather and Paw Pads:* Blue. *Eye Color:* Brilliant Copper.

CLASSIC TABBY PATTERN: Markings dense, clearly defined, and broad. Legs evenly barred with bracelets coming up to meet the body markings. Several unbroken necklaces on neck and upper chest, the more the better. Frown marks on forehead form intricate letter *M*. Unbroken line runs back from outer corner of eye. Swirls on cheeks. Vertical lines over back of head extend to shoulder markings, which are in the shape of a butterfly with both upper and lower wings distinctly outlined and marked with dots inside outline. Back markings consist of a vertical line from butterfly down the entire spine with a vertical stripe paralleling it on each side, the three stripes well separated by stripes of the ground color. Large solid blotch on each side to be encircled by one or more unbroken rings. Side markings should be the same on both sides. Double vertical row of buttons on chest and stomach.

MACKEREL TABBY PATTERN: Markings dense, clearly defined, and all narrow pencillings. Legs evenly barred with narrow bracelets coming up to meet the body markings. Necklaces on neck and chest distinct, like so many chains. Head barred with an *M* on the forehead. Unbroken lines running back from the eyes. Lines running down the head to meet the shoulders. Spine lines run together to form a narrow saddle. Narrow pencillings run around body.

PATCHED TABBY PATTERN: A Patched Tabby (Torbie) is an established silver, brown, or blue tabby with patches of red and/or cream.

BROWN PATCHED TABBY: Ground color brilliant coppery brown with classic or mackerel tabby markings of dense black with patches of red and/or cream clearly defined on both body and extremities. A blaze of red and/or cream on the face is desirable. Lips and chin the same shade as the rings around the eyes. *Eye Color:* Brilliant Copper.

BLUE PATCHED TABBY: Ground color, including lips and chin, pale bluish ivory with classic or mackerel tabby markings of very deep blue affording a good contrast with ground color. Patches of cream clearly defined on both body and extremities. A blaze of cream on the face is desirable. Warm fawn overtones or patina over the whole. *Eye Color:* Brilliant Copper.

PLATE 2

PLATE 3

SILVER PATCHED TABBY: Ground color, including lips and chin, pale silver with classic or mackerel tabby markings of dense black with patches of red and/or cream clearly defined on both body and extremities. A blaze of red and/or cream on the face is desirable. *Eye Color:* Brilliant Copper or Hazel.

SILVER TABBY: Ground color, including lips and chin, pale clear silver. Markings dense black. *Nose Leather:* Brick Red. *Paw Pads:* Black. *Eye Color:* Green or Hazel.

RED TABBY: Ground color red, Markings deep, rich red. Lips and chin red. *Nose Leather and Paw Pads:* Brick Red. *Eye Color:* Brilliant Copper.

BROWN TABBY: Ground color brilliant coppery brown. Markings dense black. Lips and chin the same shade as the rings around the eyes. Back of leg black from paw to heel. *Nose Leather:* Brick Red. *Paw Pads:* Black or Brown. *Eye Color:* Brilliant Copper.

BLUE TABBY: Ground color, including lips and chin, pale bluish ivory. Markings a very deep blue, affording a good contrast with ground color. Warm fawn overtones or patina over the whole. *Nose Leather:* Old Rose. *Paw Pads:* Rose. *Eye Color:* Brilliant Copper.

CREAM TABBY: Ground color, including lips and chin, very pale cream. Markings buff or cream, sufficiently darker than the ground color to afford good contrast but remaining within the dilute color range. *Nose Leather and Paw Pads:* Pink. *Eye Color:* Brilliant Copper.

CREAM TABBY: Ground color, including lips and chin, very pale cream. Markings buff or cream, sufficiently darker than the ground color to afford good contrast but remaining within the dilute color range. *Nose Leather and Paw Pads:* Pink. *Eye Color:* Brilliant Copper.

TORTOISESHELL: Black with unbrindled patches of red and cream. Patches clearly defined and well broken on both body and extremities. Blaze of red or cream on face is desirable. *Eye Color:* Brilliant Copper.

CALICO: White with unbrindled patches of black and red. White predominant on underparts. *Eye Color:* Brilliant Copper.

DILUTE CALICO: White with unbrindled patches of blue and cream. White predominant on underparts. *Eye Color:* Brilliant Copper.

BLUE-CREAM: Blue with patches of solid cream. Patches clearly defined and well broken on both body and extremities. *Eye Color:* Brilliant Copper.

BI-COLOR: White with unbrindled patches of black, or white with unbrindled patches of blue, or white with unbrindled patches of red, or white with unbrindled patches of cream. Cats with no more white than a locket and/or button do not qualify for this color class. Such cats shall be judged in the color class of their basic color with no penalty for such locket and/or button. *Eye Color:* Brilliant Copper.

OMC (Other Manx Colors): Any other color pattern with the exception of those showing hybridization resulting in the colors chocolate, lavender, the Himalayan pattern, or these combinations with white. *Eye Color:* Appropriate to the predominant color of the cat.

Allowable outcross breeds—None.

PLATE 4

PLATE 5

CHAPTER NINE

Interpreting the Manx Standard

Barbara St. Georges, CFA all-breed judge

It has been twenty years since I began breeding Manx cats, and it was five years before that when I became aware of them in the show ring and started to love and admire them—twenty–five years in all. And the same strong, robust, rounded-looking cat that I first saw is basically the one that exists today. The CFA Standard has been changed several times over the years, but I don't feel the changes so much affected the Manx cat as did the terminology or language of the Standard.

Trying to think of the proper words to describe any breed is difficult at best; trying to think of words to describe the Manx has taken years, for it is such a unique cat. No tail (or only a slight rise), great depth of flank, high hindquarters, and a double coat are just a few of the unusual qualities known to this breed. Many famous Manx breeders have contributed long hours and helpful ideas over the years (more recently through the CFA Manx Breed Council), but, prior to this, by sending in Standard changes to the CFA Board of Directors. It has been through their efforts and constant updating of the wording that we have the excellent Standard with which we are working today. I really feel the refinement that has come to the Manx cat over the years is due mainly to this better phraseology. For isn't the Standard really a breeder's guide on how to breed as near perfect a specimen

Above: The Manx benching row at a Las Vegas Cat Club show. Photo: Marjan Swantek. Below: CFA judge and Manx breeder Barbara St. Georges judging Ch. and Pr. Lupracan Mus Divlyn Doolish at the Fiesta City Cat Club show in Santa Barbara, CA. Breeder: Mary E. Stewart. Owner: Janelle Preston. Photo: Marjan Swantek.

PLATE 6

PLATE 7

Chanan

as possible? A Standard *is* written to describe the perfect cat in each breed.

In looking at the CFA Manx Standard, you can see in the general description that the key word in describing the Manx is *round*, or *roundness*. Fifty points, one half of the total allotted, goes to the head and the body. And look at the number of times the word *round* is used! In fact, this is the key word in the entire Standard. For if the Manx has a long body, long head, long neck, or if the cat is too fine boned, it cannot appear round. Therefore, it cannot receive enough points to conform to the Standard, and it *should not* receive Winners' ribbons because too great a number of points has been lost with these faults.

GENERAL

I think the general description is almost perfect. Even the most uninformed cat person should, on reading this description, know exactly what a Manx looks like. Besides picturing a rounded cat, he should also be able to easily picture a medium-sized, sturdy, powerful cat, firm and muscular, as so well described in both the general and body sections.

HEAD AND EARS

The Manx head is very round and jowly and there is a gentle nose dip. The ears are medium in size in proportion to the head, widely spaced, giving a "cradle" appearance known only to the Manx. The eyes are large, round, and full.

BODY

The body of the Manx is muscled and solid with sturdy bone structure. The Manx is a stout cat with a broad chest. The back should be short but in proportion to the rest of the cat. The back should arch from shoulders to rump to form the desirable round look. If the Manx is either too long bodied or too short bodied, it will not have a balanced appearance.

Another quality known only to the Manx is depth of flank. The flank is the fleshy area between the ribs and hips. The

Manx has greater depth than any other breed, causing considerable depth to the body when viewed from the side.

TAILLESSNESS, LEGS, AND FEET

The next largest amount of points after body and head goes to taillessness and legs and feet, each carrying fifteen points, and each unique in that they are *only* Manx characteristics. Complete taillessness is, of course, desired, in keeping with the look of the perfect Manx. However, in recent years, a rise has become allowable. A rise is one vertebra of tailbone and, should it be more or enough to stop a judge's hand upon examination, it becomes a penalizing fault. If the overall qualities of the Manx with a rise are better than that of a tailless specimen, the one with the rise should win.

The long, hind legs of the Manx cause its rump to be higher than its shoulders, but the rounded, muscular look applies to this area too. The legs should be heavily boned and straight, not spindly. A Manx with fine-boned legs is a strange looking cat indeed.

COAT

The coat of the Manx, worth ten points, helps to accentuate the round appearance. Not all Manx have a true double coat, and, quite often, even those that do, completely lose the cottony undercoat in the summer. This leaves them with a single, non-showable coat. Many people don't realize that a Manx can shed its coat and look just as poor as a Persian cat without its full coat, come summer.

In perfect coat, one can see the guard, or outer, hairs actually standing out from the body and, upon examination, one can see and feel the thick but soft undercoat. When in top show condition, the Manx coat should glisten with cleanliness, and good care and good health will show their rewards.

EYES, COLOR, AND MARKINGS

The least amount of points, five each, goes to the eyes and to color. Copper eye color is desired, of course, but is very difficult to come by. Gold eye color is more realistic, though

PLATE 8

PLATE 9

certainly not perfection. Least desirable are green eyes, except, of course, in the silver color shades.

As far as coat colors go, one would hope for as near to the Standard requirements as possible. But, since all the other point requirements add up so high to make the perfect Manx cat, eye and coat color can be somewhat overlooked. However, as one judge recently said when making a Manx Best in Show, "In addition to being a lovely Manx, this cat has true black smoke color . . . difficult to get in any breed of cat, but on the Manx it's like icing on a cake."

HERE TO STAY

Today the Manx is one of the most popular breeds of cats, in demand not only for its extreme intelligence and fun-loving nature, but also for its extraordinary good health and strength. Rarely seen in the show ring in the 1950's, Manx are now a common sight at cat shows throughout the United States. The finals at most shows include a Manx. Spectators in the '50's were heard to say, upon seeing a Manx, "Oh, what kind of a cat is that?" "And where is its tail?" At a recent show, I listened to numerous spectators as they looked at my Manx and all were well aware of what breed they were observing. Yes, I am proud to say the Manx is here to stay.

CHAPTER TEN

Manx of the British Isles

M anx were exhibited at the first cat shows held in England in the late 19th century, although they often had knobs or stumps and were not completely tailless. At that time, the British Manx had a rounded head and a "cradled" ear-set that tapered to a rounded point. In profile, the Manx arched from shoulder to rump and had good depth of flank. It had a double coat like that of a rabbit, with a dense undercoat and a softer outercoat. The colors were of a wide variety with corresponding eye color. British Manx had the reputation of being very intelligent, good hunters and jumpers, in spite of their lack of a tail.

The Manx Club of England was formed in 1901. One of the early champions was a tabby named Katzenjammer, belonging to Mrs. H. Brooke, while the late Sir Claude and Lady Alexander were known for their famous Ballochmyle Manx. In the 1920's and 30's the late Mrs. H. Hill Shaw owned several outstanding Manx, including Champion Finchley Boy and Katzenjammer's Ghost, the latter being considered a nearly perfect specimen. Mrs. M. Sladen, of Stoner Manx fame, also bred many champions over the years. More recently, there have been the Rosental, Brightwell, Manxtown, and Dreemskeery lines among the winners, along with the Tatleberry line from Wales. Many British Manx are exported around the world, especially to Europe where they are incorporated into the various Manx lines on the Continent.

Manx of the Isle of Man do not compete with their British relatives, but participate in their own Royal Manx shows.

PLATE 10

PLATE 11

These shows are part of the County and Regional Fairs and are housed in the "Fur and Feather" tents, along with pigeons and rabbits. The cats are stacked in tiers of cages and usually judged on a table or bench with a plaid blanket cover. Awards are similar to those in England, *i.e.*, silk rosettes and cards.

One of the more interesting cat shows that I attended in London was the Kensington Neuter and Kitten Show, where 1100 entries were housed in one large show hall. The GCCF (Governing Council of the Cat Fancy) shows are so different from American shows that I found it fascinating. The cats were benched in early morning, and when the public was admitted at 1 PM, the exhibitors had already spent half of the day in the pub below, while their cats were being judged. The cats were arranged in Class order, as listed in the catalogue; and, if you were the owner of two breeds of cats or more, they were *not* benched together, so you had to split your time with them (when you weren't in the pub, of course!). The cages were metal with very secure closures, and only white accessories could be used for pans and dishes. Additionally, a towel could be placed in the bottom of the cage.

OFFICIAL STANDARD
Governing Council of the Cat Fancy
(GCCF)

MANX

HEAD: Fairly round and large with prominent cheeks. Nose broad and straight, of medium length without break. Strong muzzle without any hint of snipyness. Firm chin and even bite.

EARS: Fairly tall, set rather high on head and angled slightly outwards. Open at base tapering to a narrow, rounded tip.

EYES: Large and round. Colour preferably in keeping with coat colour.

BODY: Solid, compact, with good breadth of chest and short back ending in a definite round rump. The rump to be higher than the shoulder. Flanks of great depth.

LEGS: Of good substance with front legs short and well set to show good breadth of chest. Back legs longer than the front with powerful, deep thighs.

COAT: Double coated showing a well padded quality arising from a short, very think undercoat and a slightly longer overcoat. The double quality of the coat is of far more importance than colour and markings, which should only be taken into account if all other points are equal. All colours and patterns are acceptable with the exception of the "Siamese" pattern.

TAILLESSNESS: Absolute taillessness is essential. The rump should be felt to be completely rounded with no definite rise of bone or cartilage interfering with the roundness of the rump.

GCCF Ch. Tatleberry Tashmentum. Breeder/owner: Jane Hellman of Wales. Photo: Sean Hellman.

PLATE 12

PLATE 13

FAULTS:
1. A rise of bone or cartilage at the end of the spine.
2. Lack of double coat.
3. Weak chin.

WITHHOLD CHALLENGE CERTIFICATES
AND FIRST PLACE IN KITTEN CLASSES FOR:
1. Definite rise of bone or cartilage at the end of the spine interfering with the roundness of the rump.
2. Uneven bite.
3. Any other anatomical abnormality (e.g., mobile or protruding xiphisternum, umbilical hernia, abnormal number of toes, etc.).

Scale of Points

Taillessness 25
Coat texture 20
Body, legs, and paws............30
Head and ears....................20
Eyes 5

Note: The GCCF Manx Standard is used in the British Isles and in Australia.

CHAPTER ELEVEN

Cattery Management
The late Lee Spafford

This chapter is written for the cat lover who aspires to breed cats as a professional rather than as a household hobbyist. Establishing a cattery involves more than just acquiring additional cats. A cattery situation presents several challenges that are not found in small-scale household breeding ventures.

Probably the most important phase in developing a cattery is planning, as most of us cat lovers tend to be motivated by emotions rather than by common sense. We must analytically decide on a maximum cattery population size and work within that limit. The number of cats you keep will figure importantly, as it will influence your decisions regarding facilities, finances, methods of health care, and other important aspects of cattery management.

Most cattery owners establish a separate area from the household as the permanent home for several of their cats. This arrangement has its advantages if (1) you like sleeping at night instead of listening to the whining of female cats in heat, (2) you like a "normal" household odor in your home (more cats means more odor), and (3) you disapprove of the habit many stud cats have of leaving romantic little "sprays" wherever they go.

There are a few things to consider here. The size of the enclosures in which you house your cats is critical to their mental and physical health, and the amount of space provided will ultimately influence the productivity of all creatures, cats included. Each cat should have a private nesting

PLATE 14

Chanan

Chanan

PLATE 15

area or box, plenty of space in which to exercise, and freedom from the mental stresses associated with overcrowding. Keep in mind that cats are not the social creatures that dogs are. The solitary nature of felines, both domestic and wild, is well documented. Cats love human compansionship, but not when it is forced upon them.

Stud cats have to be considered a separate problem. Each stud's quarters should be isolated from those of another to prevent visual agitation and nasal assaults that result from spraying to mark territories. Stud cats that are not isolated generally will be harder to handle, so they spend most of their time being irritated by the presence of other studs. Several of us can testify to the fact that even the most loving stud cat will have its cranky moments, usually at a most inopportune time.

The subject of facilities would not be complete without a mention of indoor versus outdoor considerations. Both have distinct advantages and disadvantages. Indoor catteries permit managers to have reasonable control over external parasites, simply because it is possible to treat a limited area with insecticides. However, a closed environment creates optimum conditions for the rapid spread of viral diseases. Many viruses are airborne at some stage of development and will sweep through a closed cattery in record time; numerous beloved cats have been lost as a result of this. Outdoor catteries, exposed to fresh air and breezes and not overcrowded, will present fewer viral problems in this respect. However, another problem will present itself in the form of external parasites. Fleas and ear mites will be evident in outdoor catteries in spite of the most stringent sanitary measures. Controlling these pests is a constant battle, because the assault comes from many directions. [It is worth noting here, too, that many internal parasites (worms, for example) have life cycles that include such intermediate hosts as crawling and flying insects, and cats have been known to snack on these creepy crawlers with great delight.] It is difficult to treat the great outdoors with sufficient insecticides to control a thriving flea population. As soon as the area is free of these pests, new inhabitants move in and start creating problems all over again. Fortunately, most of us don't have to agonize over the decision of indoors v. outdoors, as cattery facilities usually are dictated by existing conditions or limitations.

A prospective cattery manager should be aware that the primary difference between a household breeder and a cattery is the degree of professionalism. Visitors and prospective buyers will expect a professional, businesslike atmosphere to prevail. Appearance of the facilities, therefore, is important to a successful cattery, as it is to any successful business. Keep facilities, including litter boxes, very tidy and clean. Household breeders may change litter boxes two or three times each week, but a cattery manager should change litter boxes *twice* a day, once in the morning and again in the evening. This attitude is in keeping with the fact that visitors expect a professional to maintain a level of care that exceeds the usual. Running a business always takes a considerable amount of time and effort, and these additional efforts should be considered before you think about starting a cattery of your own.

Hired help can lighten the load a bit, but keep in mind the one most important rule for effective animal care: *Know your animals.* Hire conscientious workers, and avoid employees who exhibit a casual attitude and who might not notice minute differences in a cat's appearance or behavior that signal impending health problems. These time signals and how they are handled will be the key to effective cattery health care.

A LOOK AT SOME CATTERIES

Briar Brae In 1973, Barbara St. Georges built her fourth cattery in Bosque Farms, New Mexico. A lot of thought went into the building of this cattery, as she wanted it to be as near perfect as possible. You see, Barbara's third cattery (built in Pound Ridge, New York) was perfection on the inside, but the runs were a disaster, because of the infestation of fleas in the hot, humid summers in the East. The runs were built of wood, about four feet off the ground, and they were divided into fourteen sections and enclosed in chicken-wire. The problems came in cleaning out the runs. They were only three feet high, so

PLATE 16

Barbara had to crawl in to clean them; that meant many splinters in the knees. Also, the cats' hair got caught on the wood bottom and was difficult to get loose.

Needless to say, the outside runs in her present cattery are working beautifully. They were laid on a cement foundation and are eight feet high, so that they are easily cleaned; first they are swept out, then hosed down. The cement was laid on an angle, sloping forward so that the runs drain off easily. Briar Brae is very lucky to be free of fleas in New Mexico. Barbara has sixteen outside runs, which are two feet wide and fifteen feet long. They get full morning sun and are shaded in the afternoon. This is perfect, as summer afternoons in New Mexico can get as hot as 98 to 100 degrees. It is always cool at night, however.

Barbara's cattery is fully airconditioned and heated. There is hot and cold running water and a refrigerator/freezer. There are windows and/or doors on each side, which provide good ventilation, and there is lots of natural light. Opposite the sixteen cages with outside runs are ten more, each about five feet wide and five feet long. These are used for the queens and their kittens. When the kittens reach about six weeks of age and have had their first inoculations, they are allowed to run loose on the cattery floor for two or three hours every morning, and thus get additional exercise.

There is a double sink with a countertop, a grooming table, and lots of large, roomy cabinets. A separate small room is provided, which can be closed off from the rest of the cattery, should an isolation room be needed. There are two large cages in this room. Above all of the cages is additional storage space for airline kennels, newspaper, boxes (for kittening), and so on.

Barbara has thought of moving to Arizona or California to be closer to her children and good friends, but she has come to really love her cattery and her flea-free state, and she has decided to call New Mexico her home. She is a CFA all-breed judge and is widely known as an outstanding, long-time breeder of Manx and other cat breeds. She has bred more CFA grand champions than most breeders in the United States, and her cattery is one of which to be proud.

Nufurs. Bill and Susan Nuffer have a marvelous cattery setup in Salinas, California. Their garage, which is attached to the house, has been converted into a comfortable cattery that is much like a living room for felines and folks. It is partially carpeted and furnished with sofas, cat furniture, shelves, and scratching posts, as well as walk-in cages for mated pairs. There is plenty of room for exercise, comfort, and varied interests. The year 'round cool climate of Monterey County provides an ideal environment for producing Manx that are hardy with good double coats. By using the extent of their house and grounds, the Nuffers have organized their cattery in a manner that fits into the natural lifestyles of the animals.

Their bedroom serves as a maternity ward for the queens and their kittens. The babies are born in a queening cage located near sliding glass doors. They spend their first weeks gaining a positive and permanent feeling for humans during this time. From the bedroom, the kittens and their mamas move to the family room next to the kitchen. Here they develop relationships with other feline members of the family.

Outdoors, the whole (unaltered) males, and household pets that prefer to be outside, are housed in 400 cubic foot runs that are roofed and equipped with shelves for perching on, scratching posts, cat shelters, litter pans, automatic water dispensers, and an assortment of toys.

Since cages are a necessary part of cattery management, all of the Nuffers' cages are of the large, walk-in type. By providing this type of confinement, the males are allowed to get plenty of exercise, comfort, and human contact. The number of comfortable, livable cages lets the Nuffers keep a good supply of breeding animals, which are necessary for a genetically diverse breeding program. They also provide large, portable cages for queening or for the isolation of sick animals.

Living in the coastal areas of California also means being subject to "flea paradise," which has created the "super flea," a pest resistant to most insecticides. At long last the Nufers have discovered a way to keep the fleas at bay, although this is hard work! Once a month they bring every cat into the family room, where the linoleum floor provides an inhospitable environment for fleas. While an exterminator sprays the house, grounds, and runs, the Nuffers bathe every cat. Yes, *every* cat. After the spraying, and when the cats have dried, they powder all the cats with Sevin and return them to their quarters. This a very effective means of flea control.

All litter boxes are scooped twice daily and litter material is changed frequently. They use about 125 pounds of litter a week. They also disinfect, wash, and clean the cat areas weekly. As a result, these clean, healthy cats are a pleasure to live with.

Customers are screened carefully, and not one cat leaves the cattery without a contract that guarantees it will always be an indoor cat, it will never be declawed, and it will be returned to the cattery if it cannot be kept by the owner. The welfare of their animals is more important to the Nuffers than the loss of a sale. The distinction between home and cattery has been purposely blurred so that the quality of human and feline existence can be maintained.

Tatleberry. The Hellmans live in Wales, and their cats have the real "country life." The females can go outside when they want to; they can climb, hunt, and generally enjoy themselves while the Hellmans are at work. The cats like to go 'round the sheep and help with the gardening.

There are five breeding females that live in the house, but only in the large kitchen-living room. The rest of the house is free of cats. Of course the queens are penned when they are in heat, but aside from that, they are allowed in and out of the house during the day. They stay in at night and whenever the Hellmans are away. When Jane Hellman is mating her cats, the queen usually lives in with one of her male stud cats during her heat period. For each queen, kittening takes place in a cardboard box filled with paper, which is placed in front of the *aga* (a coal-burning stove for cooking and heating water). Jane finds that cardboard boxes provide warmth and can be easily changed and disposed of. Jane stays with her queens while they are kittening. As soon as the birth of a litter is over, the mothers settle in easily with their kittens. The kittens, as they grow, become accustomed to all that is going on. When they can climb out of the box, they begin to explore their surroundings. Once the kittens become interested in "adult food," Jane starts them on baby food, and solid food is added gradually. The mothers wean their own kittens, and this helps to produce socially well-adjusted cats.

The Hellmans have two male stud cats, Tash and Taiga, who live in outdoor houses with runs. Each one also has time outside its run for a romp with the other cats. The four houses and pens that acommodate the cats are built on a slope adjoining the Hellman's house. Taiga and Tash live at opposite ends. The middle houses are for queens that are in heat or for an occasional female that is not getting along with the others at the moment. Each cat house is built of cement blocks, faced inside and out with painted cement. The runs are built on a wooden framework, set off the ground for easy maintenance. The entrance doors are a foot above the ground, and this stops the cats from rushing out when the door is opened. There are large shelves, each of which has a removable front section into which an entrance hole has been cut. Inside is placed a cardboard box with bedding. There is a tree branch in each run, and the cats have a good view of everything. They can jump and climb and get their much needed exercise.

If there is a sick cat, it is isolated in the bathroom, which is warmed by a hot water tank, and this room serves as a "hospital." There is plenty of space in there for humans and a convalescing feline.

When the Hellmans decided to import Taiga from the United States, they had to find suitable quarantine quarters for his entry into Europe. They decided upon a "cats only" facility in Wiltshire, England, called Cheldene Quarantine Cattery.

At first Taiga did not eat as well as he had previously, but he soon adjusted to the new diet and was very much at home, spraying his quarters daily. By Christmas he was home with the Hellmans. The cats come through customs and are then transported to the quarantine cattery in a closed travelling box. They require a health certificate and must be given a rabies inoculation upon arrival to the cattery. Cheldene may be visited during the quarantined pet's stay, which is for six months' duration.

Het Huys Buytensorgh. Franklin Boon is a Manx breeder in Holland and he has two females and a neuter, International Champion Sumark van 't Huys Buytensorgh, Caroline of Ramsey (imported from the Isle of Man), and Douglas of Otrabanda (a son of Caroline).

Quintessenza. Else Lüders was the first, and probably the most important, Manx breeder in Denmark. Ten years ago she had a stumpy Manx and then imported some Manx from Man to start her fine cattery. In 1981 she was instrumental in founding the Danish Manx Club. Else has fifteen to twenty Manx and several litters each year. Many of her cats are prize winners at the shows.

Tibeert. Ad and Annelies Peyen, who live in Holland, imported a stud cat, Red Oaks Mill Mannix of Daphne, from the United States and a male from the Isle of Man. They also have three females. Mannix is the sire of Franklin Boon's Sumark.

Gijsbrecht van Aemstel. Another Dutch cattery of Henk Wellinghoff, a very enthusiastic Manx breeder. Currently he has a red tabby female and a neutered male.

Manxdrecht. The Dutch cattery of Jan and Rian Kop. They imported three Danish Manx from Else Lüders. They have a beautiful white stud that is half Danish and half American/British, named Ringo van Manxdrecht. In addition, they have four females—a rumpy, a rumpy-riser, a stumpy, and a tailed.

Golden Dimple. Another Dutch cattery, owned by Sjef and Maike Kuppen. Golden Dimple has imported five Manx from Great Britain (Jane Hellman, Tatleberry) and the United States (Barbara St. Georges, Briar Brae). Their stud is Tatleberry Eiddwen, a red tabby, and they have five females and a Cymric male, besides.

FIFé Standard
(This Manx Standard, used primarily in Europe, has been translated from German.)

BODY AND LEGS: Medium size, sturdy bone structure, lacking a tail, short back, and deep flanks are the main distinguishing characteristics of the Manx cat. Very important, also, is the round rump; round, like an orange, is ideal. The hindquarters cannot be too high and the back cannot be too short. The flanks shall be very deep. Broad chest.

COLORS: All colors are allowed, also every color variety with white. The color should be patched like bi-colors or tri-colors.

COAT: Short, outstanding texture. Double-coated, undercoat is soft and thick.

Gr. Pr. Clacritter Jared. Breeder/owner: Leslie Falteisek. Photo: F. E. Boon.

HEAD AND EARS: Relatively large and round. Strong, developed cheeks, and medium long nose without an obvious stop, but not snub-nosed (Persian type). Medium large ears, open at the base, and relatively high set and pointed.

EYES: Large, round. Eye color suited to the coat as with the British Shorthair; however, it is not so important.

NOSE LEATHER: To suit the coat color.

PAW PADS: To suit the coat color.

TAIL: On a show animal the tail must be absent. On the end of the spine, where in other cats the tail begins, there must be an indentation.

Points:

Absence of tail	25
Conformation	25
Short Back	10
Head and Ears	15
Coat	15
Eyes	5
Condition	5
TOTAL	100 points

CHAPTER TWELVE

Your Manx Cat's Health

Part of your responsibility as a Manx owner is to keep your cat healthy. A nutritionally sound diet, opportunities for exercise, and grooming assistance are important elements of health care maintenance, as are periodic trips to the veterinarian. Each year you should make an appointment with the vet for a general check-up, and at the same time you and the veterinarian should discuss a vaccination program for your cat. Vaccinations are the best form of preventive care to protect your Manx from contagious cat diseases. Following are some feline diseases and health problems of which you should be aware. These sections are not meant to be a substitute for your veterinarian; they are merely presented here so that you, as a cat owner, can become familiar with the signs of illness. Make daily observations of your Manx in an effort to establish a pattern of what is normal for your cat. If you suspect something is wrong, consult your vet to discuss the problem. It is recommended that you keep a copy of Joan O. Joshua's book, *Cat Owner's Encyclopedia of Veterinary Medicine* (T.F.H. Publications), on hand; it is an excellent reference for feline diseases.

FELINE PANLEUKOPENIA

Also known as infectious enteritis, feline distemper, cat plague, or cat fever, this highly contagious viral disease spreads so rapidly that an infected cat can weaken and die within hours. Cats of all ages are susceptible, but kittens are particularly vulnerable. This is why it is imperative that kittens be immunized soon after they have been weaned from their mother. Signs to watch for are fever, depression, weight loss, dehydration, loss of appetite, vomiting, and diarrhea. A cat or kitten may hover over its water dish, unable to drink. It may become lethargic, neglect to groom its coat, refuse to play, and it may stop eating and drinking altogether. If any of these signs are apparent, seek the assistance of your veterinarian immediately before the animal becomes severely dehydrated and emaciated.

Transmission of the panleukopenia virus can occur a number of ways, usually through direct contact with infected cats or with various items (food and water dishes, bedding, toys, cages) that have been touched by the diseased cats. Fleas also transmit the disease, as do the hands and clothing of cat handlers. Additionally, cats that have recovered may continue to shed the virus in their urine and feces for some time. The virus can also be passed from a pregnant queen to her unborn kittens by means of the placenta.

Strict sanitary measures must be taken, and sick animals must be isolated in warm, draft-free quarters until they have recovered completely. Fluids to combat dehydration, antiemetics to control vomiting, antibiotics to fight infection, and blood transfusions are given as needed to treat this dread disease. Vaccination, of course, is the most effective means of prevention. Typically, the panleukopenia vaccine is given in conjuction with the rhinotracheitis and calicivirus vaccines, a combination often referred to as the "3 in 1" shot.

UPPER RESPIRATORY DISEASES

If your Manx appears to have symptoms similar to those associated with the human cold, it may be suffering from one of the feline respiratory diseases. Those respiratory infections commonly seen are feline viral rhinotracheitis (FVR), feline calicivirus (FCV), and feline pneumonitis. The signs of illness are similar for all three of these highly contagious diseases and may include fever, sneezing, watery eyes, runny nose, mouth breathing (due to blocked nasal passages), loss of appetite, depression, and weight loss. Symptoms may range from mild to severe and they may occur alone or in combination. With FVR, frequent sneezing is most noticeable, as are thick nasal and ocular discharges. Signs of FCV may vary depending on the particular strain of calicivirus and the severity of disease in the animal. Sometimes there are few or no signs, while in severe cases the cat may exhibit pneumonia. Fever ulcers on the tongue and in the mouth are often associated with FCV. Conjunctivitis (inflammation of the eye) is seen with pneumonitis, which is caused by the agent *Chlamydia psittaci*.

Transmission of upper respiratory diseases occurs when infected cats sneeze and spray virus-containing secretions into the air. Handlers of cats can also spread these viral diseases, as can recovered cats who may shed the particular virus in their saliva or feces. Needless to say, cats that are closely confined in a multi-cat household or cattery are particularly susceptible. Vaccination, therefore, is extremely important, not only for all feline members of one's family—especially young kittens—but even for singly-kept pets who may come in contact with other cats. Treatment involves preventing further spread of infection by keeping infected cats isolated in clean, warm, well-ventilated (but draft-free) areas. It is vitally important to encourage a sick cat to eat by enticing it with a variety of strongly flavored foods, since its sense of smell may be hindered due to nasal blockage. Antihistamines will probably be prescribed to help dry the nasal passages and, in severe cases, antibiotics may be indicated for infection.

FELINE LEUKEMIA VIRUS

Probably the most dreaded disease in catdom, the feline leukemia virus (FeLV) is a highly contagious immunosuppressive disease; that is to say, it impairs a cat's natural immune system, interfering with the animal's ability to fight off not only the leukemia but other diseases as well. With the immune system inhibited, the cat becomes increasingly vulnerable to other viral and bacterial diseases and infections, among them feline infectious peritonitis. FeLV may be directly or indirectly related to various respiratory, reproductive, digestive, and skin problems, and many times when a cat does not respond to treatment for a particular condition, FeLV is suspected.

Not all cats exposed to the feline leukemia virus will succumb to the disease; many will develop an immunity and many won't be affected by the disease at all. Most cats that are diagnosed as having FeLV, those that are FeLV-positive, die within just a few years' time, although some infected cats do improve and carry the disease for years without showing obvious symptoms. The danger is that these seemingly healthy carriers may infect other cats with which they come in contact, cats who are free of the virus. Those cats that have been exposed to the virus but which test negative may have developed immunity to the disease, but it is wise to have a cat re-tested from time to time just to make certain it is not harboring the virus.

Since FeLV is often linked with other diseases and problems, it may be difficult to detect in its early stages. The signs of illness may be quite varied and may include any of the following: fever, depression, anemia, loss of appetite, weight loss, jaundice, vomiting, diarrhea, lethargy, or breathing difficulty. A recurring or persistent fever, illness, or infection may indicate the presence of the leukemia virus, which interferes with red blood cell production. The "fading kitten syndrome," whereby a kitten has difficulty nursing, fails to gain weight, and steadily weakens, is often associated with FeLV.

Transmission occurs largely by means of the saliva when, for example, an infected cat bites, licks, or rubs another cat with its mouth or tongue, and feeding dishes shared by several cats may also be a nidus of infection. Besides being shed in the saliva, the virus can also be shed in the urine, feces, milk, and nasal secretions; therefore, it is possible for the virus to be transmitted to a cat that comes in contact with the contaminated urine and feces of an infected cat (at the litter box, perhaps), and it is conceivable for nursing kittens to receive the virus through their mother's milk if she is a FeLV-carrier. It is also thought by some experts that the virus may be transmitted through sneezing and also by such blood-sucking parasites as fleas, as the flea bites an infected cat and then a noninfected one.

Check with your veterinarian about testing your Manx for FeLV and vaccinating him. Some things to consider are the number of cats in your household, whether the cats are indoor or outdoor cats, and the history of FeLV among your household cats.

FELINE INFECTIOUS PERITONITIS

Much research has been conducted, but at this time there is no known cure for the progressively debilitating disease, feline infectious peritonitis (FIP). Caused by a coronavirus, the disease can be difficult to detect because there are other coronaviruses seen in cats and these resemble the one responsible for producing FIP. Diagnosis can also be tough because many cats with FIP are also infected with feline leukemia virus, which suppresses the animal's immune system. Cats of all ages are susceptible, although cats younger than two years usually become victims. The incidence of FIP is high where many cats live in close association (catteries, multi-cat households) and where noninfected cats frequently come in contact with infected cats' saliva, feces, urine, and respiratory secretions. And, as is the case with other contagious viral diseases, there may be carrier cats who shed the virus but who themselves show no signs of illness. Death is not always the outcome for those cats diagnosed with FIP; the disease can go into remission, especially if detected early.

There are two forms of FIP seen, the "wet" form being more prevalent. Fever, weight loss, breathing difficulty, a distended abdomen (result of fluid build-up), lethargy, and loss of appetite are signs to watch for. The animal may seem to be uncomfortable most of the time and may refuse to be handled. With the "dry" form, however, signs of illness are not so obvious; there may be fever or no signs at all. Examination of the internal organs, such as the kidneys and liver, and lymph nodes reveal inflammation if the dry form of FIP is present.

FELINE INFECTIOUS ANEMIA

Caused by the organism *Hemobartonella felis*, feline infectious anemia (FIA) can affect cats of all ages. The disease is often associated with stress or other diseases, such as feline leukemia virus or feline infectious peritonitis. Signs of hemobartonellosis may include high fever, depression, loss of appetite, weight loss, rapid breathing, and, in severe cases, jaundice. Your Manx may seem weak and listless, and its normally pink-colored gums may appear white or blue. The veterinarian will probably recommend that a blood smear be done to see if the *H. felis* organism is present in the cat's system, and blood transfusions probably will be given in severe cases. Since it is believed that transmission occurs through fleas and ticks, which suck their hosts' blood, eradication of these parasites from the cat and its environment is crucial.

CONJUNCTIVITIS

If you notice inflammation, infection, or swelling around one or both of your cat's eyes, the animal may be suffering from conjunctivitis, which can develop for a variety of reasons. Most cases of conjunctivitis involve viruses associated with upper respiratory diseases, and probably the most common cause of the inflammation is the *Chlamydia psittaci* organism associated with pneumonitis. Other forms of conjunctivitis may be caused by the herpesvirus seen in feline rhinotracheitis, another upper respiratory disease. A purulent discharge from the eyes is often seen and sometimes there may be corneal ulceration. Eye injuries, allergies, dust, or foreign bodies may also cause the conjunctivitis to form. Your veterinarian will probably prescribe eye drops or an antibiotic ointment to treat the problem. Most cats recover completely with proper treatment.

GINGIVITIS

Gingivitis, or inflammation of the gums, is common among cats, no matter what the breed. In the eighteen years that I have been breeding Manx, this problem has occurred more frequently than any other, so I feel it is important to mention it here. What happens is that tartar builds up on the cat's teeth; if left untreated, bacterial infection and inflammation can set in. A sure method of prevention is to offer dry cat food to your Manx. These convenient particles can be left out in a small dish for a few days without spoiling. Chewing on the dry food exercises the gums and helps keep tartar from forming and getting out of hand. It is a way for cats to "brush" their teeth the way we do ours with a toothbrush. But besides offering dry food, you need to take the cat to your veterinarian periodically so that he or she can scale the animal's teeth, i.e., remove the dental tartar.

EPILEPSY

Having had a Manx that experienced seizures brings me close to the problem of epilepsy, which is not common but which can be seen in cats. Epilepsy is not a disease, rather it is a state of repetitive convulsions or seizures brought on by various causes (head trauma or injury, a brain tumor, encephalitis), and the signs can vary from very mild to severe. There may be a temporary loss of consciousness, i.e., a "blacking out" or fainting, the cat may seem apprehensive and may not recognize its owner, it may be unresponsive to normal stimuli, or it may seem disoriented and glassy-eyed. The seizures sometimes occur when the cat is at rest or asleep. My Manx would go into uncontrolled spasms, flop around, and thrash her body in different directions for a few minutes; when the fit was over, her heart would be racing and she would seem confused. I remember she would meow quite a bit and then go straight to her food dish, as though food were a secure refuge after a very startling experience. My veterinarian prescribed a medicine to control the seizures, and after experimenting with dosage, I am happy to report that my cat lives a normal, healthy life . . . as long as she is medicated. It should be mentioned here that there is no cure for this disorder, but with some cats, epilepsy can be controlled with proper treatment, as advised by a veterinarian.

MEGACOLON

When large fecal masses form in the cat's colon (intestines), they may form an impaction and the animal will have difficulty with defecation. Your veterinarian will probably want to know if your Manx has a history of severe constipation and will want to know what type of diet is being offered. An enema may be needed to remove the mass, and a high fiber diet recommended. Cymrics, the longhaired Manx, will need regular grooming attention, particularly in the anal region. The long hair in this area may become matted if it is not brushed often; if the matted hair combines with any fecal matter, the result might be a barrier to the passage of the feces. Megacolon is not exclusively a Manx problem; however, it does occur in our breed more frequently than in others. The abnormal fused sacral vertebrae and pelvic bones sometimes create an anal opening so small that constipation/and problems with defecation can result.

RABIES
Make sure you check with your veterinarian about having your Manx vaccinated against this dread disease, to which, by the way, *all* warm-blooded animals—including man—are susceptible. Vaccination is the best form of protection for your cat, because once rabies has been contracted, there is no cure. Dogs typically have been vaccinated for rabies because in most places it is required by law; however, this has not been the case with domestic felines. The result in the past few years is that there has been an increase in the number of feline rabies victims.

Many wild animals, such as raccoons, skunks, foxes, bats, and even rabbits and squirrels, have been known to carry rabies. If your Manx is bitten, scratched, or even licked by one of these animals which may be carrying the disease, there could be problems if your cat has not been immunized with a rabies vacccine. The rabies virus is transmitted through the saliva of a rabid animal.

There are two types of rabies seen. With "dumb" rabies, the victim usually suffers from paralysis and is characterized by a drooping jaw. Soon other limbs and organs become paralyzed and death follows shortly. Cats that exhibit "furious" rabies, on the other hand, sometimes foam at the mouth and are said to be "mad." There may be a sudden change in behavior where a normally shy cat becomes aggressive or a cat

The friendly, pleasant look of Divlyn Doolish typifies the Manx expression. Breeder: Mary E. Stewart. Owner: Janelle Preston. Photo: Chanan.

that is usually friendly becomes nasty, biting and snapping at anyone who comes near him.

In summary, two warnings are given to all Manx owners with regard to rabies: have your cat vaccinated and never allow it to roam into areas where wild animals that may be carriers of rabies lurk.

CHAPTER THIRTEEN

Breeding Your Manx

Breeding Manx cats is fascinating and it can be a real challenge because of the tailless factor associated with the breed. One can find all sorts of surprises in a litter—rumpies, rumpy-risers, and Manx with various tail lengths from stumpies to longies to tailed! Then, of course, one must consider the deformities which can and do result. It seems the better the specimen (in terms of the breed standard), the more likely deformities will show up. Unless novices have the guidance of veteran Manx breeders behind them, the breeding of these wonderful cats can be a great disappointment. Manx are interesting and entertaining pets, and breeding good-quality specimens can be so rewarding. I really consider myself more of a Manx fancier than a true breeder since I keep so few cats. I do not breed for purposes of showing my cats but rather for people interested in owning a pet Manx. I prefer to promote the breed itself rather than to promote my own cats or my cattery reputation.

SELECTING A MATE

Like most cat breeders, Manx breeders search for suitable mates for their cats, mates that show strengths where their own cats show weaknesses. For example, if a Manx has a poor earset (placement of the ears), a breeder will look for a mate with an excellent earset to compensate for their cat's lack of this desirable trait. In this way the offspring of the mating will carry the desired earset trait and pass it along to successive generations in the line. If you plan to breed your female, seek the services of a Manx stud (a male breeder cat) that is producing good offspring. Go to cat shows. Talk to

Manx breeders. Find out all you can about those cats that are winning at the shows. Examine the pedigrees of these top show-quality Manx. Study the genetic histories of the lines you plan to breed into. Remember that the breeding pair should complement each other and produce even better kittens than they themselves were.

If you own a male Manx that will be used for stud service, he will need quarters of his own. Most male cats tend to "mark their territory" by spraying urine on various objects and in various places. Even if he does not spray, he will definitely have a strong male odor once he starts siring. Breed your stud only to females with complementary type to insure offspring which exhibit those Manx features that you want to propagate. Oftentimes the owner of the stud will take a pick-of-the-litter kitten in place of a stud fee, but details of the breeding agreement should be worked out well in advance of the actual mating.

MATING

Usually the stud is brought to the queen (a female breeder cat) so that she stays in heat in her own familiar surroundings. The Manx stud seems to perform almost anywhere, so it is easier to transport him to his mate. Whether the stud goes to the queen or vice versa really depends, among other things, upon the breeding quarters available. If all goes well, it will take only a few days for the queen to conceive, and, hopefully, after approximately a nine-week gestation period, live kittens will be the end result. Litter sizes vary, but usually three to five kittens can be expected as the average. If you leave the mating pair together for too long a time, it may be difficult to determine the exact conception date. And, if the kittens were conceived at different intervals during the queen's heat cycle, at birth they may not all be at the same level of maturity. Incidentally, even though most queens will scream out during copulation, due to the tiny barb-like projections on the stud's penis, this is not the case all of the time. I had one queen that was so quiet while she was in heat and while being bred that I had to put her in with a stud for

114

quite some time and hope! I had to guess at the due date and just sit back and wait eagerly.

SOME THINGS TO CONSIDER

There are some things you should be aware of when breeding Manx cats. The gene for taillessness is a lethal one and is responsible for producing dead or deformed kittens. This is why rumpy-to-rumpy breedings are seldom employed; this is also why the Manx is not considered genetically pure, that is to say, it does not breed true. When you study the genetic history of the cat to which your own Manx will be bred, notice if there is a predominance of rumpy grand champions. If there is, this may mean that there are several generations of more extreme-type cats than you may want in your kittens' background. Plan to include a tailed ancestor in the breeding plan or at least something more than just rumpies for several generations; otherwise, you are sure to run into problems . . . stillborn kittens or kittens which may have difficulty standing, walking, or controlling their sphincter muscles. All sorts of skeletal deformities, including varying degrees of spina bifida, may pop up.

Skeletal abnormalities, by the way, are not just linked to taillessness. The pelvis is frequently involved and may appear shortened, or the sacral bones may fuse together. The pelvis may be tipped or the spinal column may not be completely closed, leaving the spinal cord unprotected. Some Manx have problems with mobility and seem to hop as a result of their inability to exercise control over the movements of their hind legs. Others may be completely paralyzed; these poor victims, however, usually die soon after birth. Intestinal problems may be seen too. Some individuals suffer from occasional or chronic constipation because of a narrowed anal opening. Many Manx kittens have recurring bouts with diarrhea after they have been weaned from their mother, although most of these kittens respond favorably to medical treatment and a change in diet. Those unfortunate Manx that are unable to control elimination of their excreta usually do not do well, and if this is the case they should be euthanized.

Some Manx experience reproductive failure and tend to resorb their young. Resorption means that the embryo dissolves and, in part, is absorbed into the bloodstream . . . thus, no kittens. Progesterone may have to be given to queens that continue to abort their young. This hormone not only sustains pregnancy but it tends to increase litter size and decrease the size of each kitten. I do not recommend giving any sort of durg to a pregnant queen unless it is a life-threatening situation; in this case, a qualified veterinarian should be consulted. Because Manx are difficult to breed, on account of the many deformities that are associated with them, this is best left to the serious fanciers and professional breeders.

There are several breeding strategies which can be employed in the breeding of Manx cats. Inbreeding, the mating of close relatives (mother to son or father to daughter, for example) is used to "lock in" or "fix" certain desirable traits. Breeders can usually predict with certainty what the offspring will look like. Unfortunately, too much close inbreeding can reduce the vigor of a particular line and undesirable characteristics can show up as well. Carefully monitored inbreeding programs and selective breeding, however, can produce successful results. Linebreeding, the mating of relatives that are not so close (niece to uncle, granddaughter to grandsire, and so on) seems to work well with Manx. This method is often used to maintain and gradually improve a line or strain. Another popular method is outcrossing, whereby a breeder tries to bring in a desired trait from another line or strain of Manx. There is more risk involved, since you are dealing with unrelated cats and it is difficult to predict the outcome of these kinds of matings; however, if pedigrees are studied with great care and if all animals that are to be mated are examined carefully, good results can be achieved.

PREGNANCY

If the mating between the stud and your queen was successful, you will notice your Manx mother-to-be growing larger over the course of her nine-week gestation period. A few weeks into the pregnancy you will notice that her nipples have become quite stiff and bright pink in color. Some females, however, don't give this nipple sign right away, rather later on when their mammary glands begin to swell in preparation for milk production. The queen's appetite will increase, so consult with your veterinarian about a special diet for her. I usually give my queens healthy portions of cottage cheese or cheddar cheese and I add a canned food fortified with extra calcium to her diet during the latter part of her pregnancy and into her nursing phase. Of course, as is the case with us humans, individual queens vary in their habits. One of my queens, for example, insisted on running over to her food dish for a quick bite to eat right before she was about to deliver her kittens. Others won't eat at all on the day they are about to give birth.

A week or so before the kittens are due, introduce your queen to her own nesting box. A fairly large, sturdy cardboard box will do, or if you are handy, one can be constructed of wood. Furnish the box with some nesting material, either newspapers or some old laundered rags or an old blanket that you won't mind cleaning later or dispoing of. Place the box in a warm, dry, draft-free spot that is dimly lit and away from all of the household commotion. Let your queen become accustomed to spending time in her nesting box so that on the big day (or during the big night is more accurate in this context!) she will give birth there. If you do not provide her with her own delivery quarters, she will probably choose her own, such as the middle of your bed or atop a pile of clothes in the laundry basket! I had success in offering some of my queens their pet carriers, the ones I use when I transport them to a cat show or to the vet. These seemed cozy enough, especially after I adorned them with a layer of nice soft bedding.

DELIVERY OF THE KITTENS

When birth is imminent, the queen may become restless and spend more time in her nesting chamber. She may want you to be near at hand for support. Let me tell you, on several occasions I have spent the night on the floor propped up against a pillow right next to my own bedroom closet, waiting for the big moment! If you can set your queen up in a cage with wheels, one that can be rolled right into your bedroom, so much the better. Position it the way you would a baby's crib. Whatever arrangements you make, do them ahead of time so that the kittens will be born in a controlled area. Don't let your queen wander off to some obscure part of the house where you won't be able to look in on the family to see all is well. And, by all means, don't let her give birth in her litter pan—altough some queens have been known to try this!

I have been lucky with my queens who have had little trouble kittening. Most of mine were short-bodied, so this was an advantage. There was one short-bodied female, though, that had some trouble giving birth; after two caesarean sections and only one live kitten, I had her spayed. I might mention that she went on to be a national CFA winner. As previously discussed, reproductive failure can occur with some Manx; others may be quite capable of producing live, healthy kittens but they may have difficulty expelling the kittens from the reproductive tract.

Make certain you stay with your queen as she delivers her young, just in case she needs your assistance. Each kit will be born in a fluid-filled amniotic sac which the mother will tear open and later consume. After she tears open the sac, she will begin to quickly lick and clean her newborn kitten. The licking helps remove fluids from the youngster's mouth and nostrils and at the same time helps stimulate breathing and circulation of blood. She will then sever the umbilical cord by biting it. (*Note:* In a few days the stump left where the cord was detached will eventually dry up and fall off.) The queen will do this for each kitten that is born. If she fails to tear open the sac or lick the kitten, you must intervene and help her. Make sure the kit finds a teat and starts to nurse. Then sit back and await the birth of the next kit. I should mention here that sometimes my male Manx like to participate in the kittening event, even if it means offering a paw or giving vocal support. They are indeed concerned about the birth of the litter, particularly if the queen is one that they know well, *and* if they have sired the litter.

If during delivery of the kittens, or afterwards when they are nursing, anything at all should go wrong, call your veterinarian immediately.

TAIL DOCKING

Within a few hours of birth, you may decide to dock the tails on some of the stumpies or longies. Since it is sometimes difficult to sell tailed Manx, most breeders dock the tails shorter so that the animals will be more acceptable to buyers. Often breeders will mention to their prospective buyers whether the tails of their Manx being offered for sale have been docked or not, particularly if any of the animals are intended for breeding. The tail length, before docking, figures importantly in the breeding scheme because it probably will influence the buyer's choice of a mate for their cat. In other words, if you buy a Manx whose tail was docked to give it a better appearance and you want to breed this cat sometime in the future, you should know that the animal carries the tailed trait in its genes. Breeders will often mention tail docking right on the animal's pedigree.

Even grand champion rumpies (that is, those with the more extreme type) can produce kittens with varying tail lengths although they themselves are tailless. I have found that there is no real consistency in successive litters produced by the same parents. It is that old "bran barrel" theory of not knowing what tail length you can expect until each kitten is born. A top-winning Manx may have a "year of the tail" and then turn around and produce several rumpy kittens. I had one Manx male with extreme type (a rumpy with a short back) who sired several litters of tailed offspring. Only one good rumpy in the whole lot! Some stud-queen combinations seem to result in a high rumpy ratio, but this is largely a matter of trial and error.

GROWTH PATTERN FOR KITTENS
BIRTH. Kittens weigh around three ounces, although one
large kitten will weigh more than several in a litter. Their eyes are closed and they are deaf.

2 WEEKS. Kittens weigh around nine ounces and open their eyes (usually five to ten days). Vision is limited, so keep them in soft light and avoid taking photographs with a flash attachment. They begin to hear.

4 WEEKS. Kittens weigh around one pound and begin to grow baby teeth. They may become interested in other food besides their mother's milk.

6 WEEKS. Kittens weigh about one-and-one-half pounds and have all of their baby teeth.

8 WEEKS. Kittens weigh around two pounds and are sometimes old enough to go to new homes. Tailed Manx are usually stronger and can be placed with new owners at this early age; others may need to wait until they are about three months old. They should be given their kitten shots now by the vet.

4 MONTHS. Kittens weigh around four pounds and eat three times a day.

6 MONTHS. Females are old enough to be spayed; however, you may choose to wait until they are seven months old.

8 MONTHS. Females will probably have their first heat period, although some may delay as long as one year. Males are often old enough to be neutered, but you may want to wait until they are nine months old. (You should have a male altered before he starts spraying everything in sight to mark his territory.)

6-12 MONTHS. Males reach their sexual maturity.

1 YEAR. Weight will vary, although males will still be heavier than females. Females usually range between eight and twelve pounds; males may range between twelve and eighteen pounds in later years. Both males and females eat once or twice a day, and they are both old enough to be bred if this is what you have in mind for them.

REMARKS FROM A MANX BREEDER

The following comments were written by Barbara St. Georges, noted Manx breeder (cattery prefix Briar Brae) and long-time CFA all-breed judge. Barbara has judged cats in

Germany, Australia, and Japan, as well as in her own country, the United States. She has numerous grand champions to her credit and has sold her Manx to people all over the world.

I have found that of the three breeds of cats I work with, the Manx make the best mothers. They are the most devoted to their litters and seem to remain with their young much longer than the other breeds I have. I don't have a Manx mother who wouldn't willingly accept kittens from another queen in an emergency situation, even a different breed of kitten. Old "Jo Ann" so loves kittens that I need only say "Do you want babies?" and she will jump in her box in the hope I will give her some. One of "Zero's" daughters, "Millie Manx," wanted kittens so badly that she used to leap twenty feet off our balcony to get bred by any visiting tom! It took me several rounds of this experience to discover how she was getting out of the house. Then one day I saw her making the leap. The resulting litter produced two kittens, both adorable but completely unlike a Manx. We named them "Romeo" and "Juliet" for the balcony scene and were fortunate enough to find homes for both of them. Once caged, "Millie Manx" produced some fine litters of Manx. She met an untimely death, however, one day when she had a stroke and now lies in peaceful repose on our hillside with "Trauntail Christopher" and several other prized Manx who have gone on to greener pastures.

When I was breeding Persians exclusively, I was taught by many who had years of experience in breeding cats that one should breed a Persian once a year only—that it was just too hard on them to breed any more often. I try never to breed a queen before ten or eleven months, but find I cannot hold them off a longer time. Then almost as soon as they have their litters, they are back in season and most of them stay in this state until they are bred again. I have found the best results come from weaning their kittens when they are eight weeks old and giving the queen a one-to-two month rest before I breed her again.

My ten Manx queens range in age from one year to ten years and all are in the best of health and condition. Manx seem to be one of the strongest breeds of cats as far as being able to stand cold weather and maintain robust health. My Manx actually enjoy sitting outside in their runs in a snow-storm. I've watched them darting about trying to catch snowflakes and even playing hide and seek in the accumulating drifts. I have never had a Manx catch cold or have any other ill effect from this sort of exposure.

I have noticed they are very true to their own kind. When a new Manx queen comes in for breeding, my three studs all spot her at one time and are very enthralled with the new arrival. However, if a Siamese or Persian queen comes, they ignore her completely. Gr. Ch. "Briar Brae Maxie" would viciously attack another breed if I let him near it, even a queen in season. But put a Manx queen in with him, and he is a real "Rudolph Valentino." When I first started working with Manx, I thought it would be fun to name them with names that begin with the letter M. We have just about used up all the names in the English language that begin with M, so I quess we'll have to start using German, French, and Italian names. However, it really made the Manx I have bred stand out namewise, and my family has had many fun hours naming cats.

I cannot write enough about the charming and comical personality of the Manx. They talk with a Brrrrrrrrrrrrp noise that is utterly charming, either in response to a person's voice or when they are amusing themselves in play. My husband's cat, Ch. "Briar Brae Matthew," better known as "Tootie," talks incessantly and truly is a companion and friend. He follows Mr. St. G. everywhere, even up onto the bathroom vanity where he Brrrrrrrrps his approval or disapproval of every move my husband makes while shaving, brushing his teeth, etc. This cute noise reaches its real peak when a queen has her kittens. Sometimes when I have three or four queens, each with a litter of kittens, the noise sounds almost like a petshop full of canaries.

The Manx at any age seem to play harder, jump higher, and have a bigger bag full of pranks and tricks than one could ever imagine. They are inventive and clever, and each day brings with it a new trick or game they have invented.

CHAPTER FOURTEEN

The Cymric

Cymrics are moderately longhaired, tailless cats that come from Manx parentage. They are *not* the result of crossing Manx with Persians or Maine Coon cats; rather, they are found spontaneously in an otherwise shorthaired litter born of shorthaired Manx parents. By breeding two longhaired Manx together, you will get only longhaired Manx.

The word *Cymric* (pronouced *kim' rick*) means *Welsh*, due to the fact that many longhaired Manx were observed in Wales at one time. From the research that I have done on the Isle of Man, it is my opinion that the longhaired gene of the Norwegian Forest Cat, brought to the Isle by King Magnus of Norway, was passed on to the British Shorthair breed, then carried forth in the tailless mutations that later ocurred on that island.

The silky, medium-length, graduated coat of the Cymric is the result of combining the longhair gene with the polygenes that modify the length of down and awn hairs. The recessive longhair gene must be present in *both* shorthaired parents (Manx) in order to produce Cymric offspring. When Cymrics mate, they produce only longhaired kittens.

When I first began breeding Manx in 1965, I would see Althea Frahm exhibiting her longhaired Manx at cat shows, calling them Manx mutations. I remember seeing her Lovebunny's Precocious Dream, a copper-eyed white male, on exhibit, as well as her Lovebunny's Smudge, an enormous black male. They often appeared in competition in American Cat Association (ACA) shows and on exhibit at CFA shows that I attended long ago. By 1975, according to an article by

Leslie Falteisek in *Daphne Negus's Cat World* magazine ("What is a Cymric?"), several cat registering associations had granted registration to longhaired Manx, and some of these cats were allowed to be shown, competing with their shorthaired brothers and sisters for Best of Breed ribbons. Many of the breeders involved with Cymrics in the early 1970's wanted a separate class for these longhaired felines. In 1976, an independent Cymric group was formed, the United Cymric Association. In May of that same year, through the efforts of Blair Wright, a Canadian Cat Association (CCA) breeder, the Cymric was accepted for championship by the CCA. In 1977, CFA changed its breed classification of longhaired Manx, limiting parentage only to registered shorthaired Manx and longhaired Manx out of registered shorthaired Manx. Before that time, the registry was open to Manx/Persian hybrids. Since many of the Manx lines used today already carry the recessive longhair gene, there is no need to introduce Persians for coat length. Using Persian cats in a Manx/Cymric breeding program would change the moderate coat length and, most definitely, the Manx type.

Many early Manx breeding programs included some Cymrics. Leslie's article, which appeared in the November-December, 1983 issue, listed many prominent Manx that produced Cymrics, including several well-known Briar Brae, Kelsha, Lupracan Mus, and Venda Manx. I, myself, had been breeding shorthaired Manx for seventeen years before I matched up the right Venda-backed female to a longhair-producing Briar Brae male. In a litter of five, one male turned out to be a Cymric. It wasn't obvious at first. Everyone kept saying, "What a nice, plushy coat this one has!" I did agree, noticing how different his coat was. In three week's time, however, I finally realized that he was a Cymric. I fell in love immediately, and ever since decided to breed these gorgeous creatures exclusively.

Some of the Cymric breeder cats that have helped develop the Cymric breed are: Sinleo's Tuffy Mouse of Arrow (brown tabby male), Plahn's Pedal Pusher of Clacritter (tortie female), Plahn's MacDuff of Maxmar (black male), Clacritter

Jason (red mackerel tabby male), Gentilbelle Jennifer, Sinleo's Hel 'n Wheels of Clacritter, Twillshire's Sassi of Maxmar, Maxmar's Polar Frost, Helle's Polar King of Maxmar, and Helle's Comus Jupiter (the first CCA Canadian Cymric grand champion).

While Cymrics are recognized for championship by most cat registering associations, they are still shown in the AOV (any other variety) class by the CFA. More and more Cymrics are being bred and shown, and we hope that soon they will be accepted in their own championship class, right alongside their shorthaired littermates.

CCA CYMRIC SHOW STANDARD
(*Canadian Cat Association*)

Revised Cymric Show Standard approved by CCA Board of Directors on September 21, 1984. Effective October 4, 1984.

GENERAL—The Cymric is a tailless, moderately longhaired cat of medium size. The sturdy, compact body is almost "bear-like" in the top specimen. The Cymric has a fair-sized, rounded head which conforms with the short, stocky body, deep flanked, heavy boned and broad at the hindquarters. Emphasis is on the well-balanced cat. Males are usually larger, with proportionately larger and slightly longer bodies and heavier bone. Cymrics walk normally. The double coat of the Cymric is a silky, soft, open one. The longer coat, the guard hairs, should be about 2–3 inches long, with a soft under or "awn" coat half the length in proportion to the guard hairs. The coat appears full, especially around the breeches, jowls and ruff. The corresponding, perfect eye colour should be considered a "plus" factor when all other points are equal. The Cymric is slow in maturing and allowance should be made in young cats in judging coat length, jowliness, ear set, shortness of front legs, and depth of flank.

POINT ALLOTMENT:

Head 25

        Size.................................... 5
        Shape 10
        Eyes................................. 5
        Ears 5

Body 40

        Width........................... 10
        Arch 10
        Length 10
        Depth of Bone................ 10

Legs and Feet... 10

        Front 5
        Back 5

Coat 20

        Length 10
        Texture 10

Condition and Balance 5

Total... 100

DESCRIPTION:

HEAD (15)—The rounded head should be slightly longer than it is broad, with a moderately rounded forehead, prominent cheek bones, and jowliness (more evident in adult male). Well-developed squarish muzzle with prominent whisker pads; there should be a definite break at the whiskers. Chin to be firm and in a straight line with the nose when viewed from the side; a weak chin is a serious fault. The nose is slightly longer than broad, and in profile there is a gentle nose dip. The neck is short and sturdy. *Objection*—Deep dip in profile (nose break); short, flattened muzzle; tapered muzzle.

EYES (5)—Large, round and full eyes are set at a slight angle downward toward the nose. The ideal colour conforms with the requirements of the colour of the coat, but in Cymrics should be considered only if all other points are equal. *Objection*—Eye-set straight across in head; bulging eyes.

EARS (5)—Ears are medium in size, rather wide at the base, and tapering gradually to a rounded tip with full, long feather-like furnishings inside. Ears are rather widely spaced and are set slightly outward and forward. Ear-tip tufts are desirable, setting off the unique Cymric-look. The shape of the ears, when viewed from behind, is that of a cradle-rocker. *Objection*—Ears set close together and/or high on head.

BODY (40)

Width (10)—The Cymric should be wide and solid-looking when viewed from above. Sturdy and hefty at the hips; broader in this area than at the shoulders. Deep, broad chest; well-sprung ribs. Flank (fleshy area of the side between ribs and hips) has greater depth than in other breeds when viewed from the side.

Arch (10)—Medium-sized body, with a short back that arches up in a gradual but continuous curve from the shoulder blades to the haunches. Rump should be round (the very long hair in this area may detract from the visual appearance of roundness, slightly). There is no penalty for a rise of bone or cartilage which does not stop the judge's hand when the palm is stroked down the back and over the rump. No probing of the dimple or rise by the judge is allowed.

Length (10)—Length of back should be approximately the same length as the hindlegs, but no longer.

Depth of Bone (10)—Good, sturdy bone structure; there should be no suggestion of spindly or delicate bone anywhere in the cat. *Objections:*—Rangy, or long-looking back; arch that does not follow a continuous upward curve; level back; visible rise or stub; narrow chest, rib cage, hips; light bone.

LEGS (10)

Front (5)—Sturdy, heavily-boned forelegs set wide apart their entire length. Feet round, firm and tufted. *Objection*—Legs too close together; long front legs same length as hindlegs.

Back (5)—The hindlegs, much longer than the front, make the rump higher than the shoulders. The heavily-boned hindlegs have heavy muscular thighs and are straight when viewed from behind. Feet round, firm and tufted. *Objections*—Short hindlegs, bowed or cowhocked (knock-kneed) hindlegs; uneven boning between front and back legs.

COAT (20)

Coat Length (10)—The open double coat should be of moderate length over the main body, gradually lengthening from shoulders to rump. Breeches, abdomen and neck ruff are longer than on the main body. The jowls should be lynx-like, and the collar-like ruff extends from the shoulder blades, bib-like, around the chest area of the cat. Breeches should be full and thick to the hocks in the mature Cymric. Lower leg and head coat (except for cheeks and neck ruff) should be dense and shorter than body coat. Toe tufts are desirable. Seasonal and age variations should be recognized. All coat colours are recognized as per Cymric colour standard. Winners are not withheld for buttons or lockets.

Coat Texture (10)—Coat texture is soft and silky. *Objections:* "In-between" coat length, that is, a coat which is slightly longer than a Manx, but could be mistaken for a short-hair until touched; overall even-length coat; thin coat; a cottony-textured coat.

CONDITION AND BALANCE (5)—The overall appearance should be that of a medium-sized, compact cat, well-fleshed, but not fat. Sturdy and muscular and surprisingly heavy when lifted. The head, neck, body and legs should blend smoothly to form a well-balanced cat.

WITHHOLD AWARDS—Coat: Too thin; too short. Condition: Underweight, overweight, soft. Tail: Stub or rise that spoils the appearance of taillessness. Colours: Other than those in the Cymric colour standard.

DISQUALIFY—Walking with hopping, hopping only; stiffness or weakness in one or both hindlegs. Evidence of hybridization resulting in the colours chocolate, lavender, Himalayan pattern ticked tabby pattern, or these combinations with white.